Super-ferries
of Britain, Europe and Scandinavia

Super-ferries of Britain, Europe and Scandinavia

Russell Plummer

PSL

PATRICK STEPHENS LIMITED

First published in 1988

British Library Cataloguing in Publication Data

Plummer, Russell
    Super-ferries : of Britain, Europe and Scandinavia.
    1. Passenger ships — Europe   2. Ferries —
    Europe
    I. Title
    623.8'234'094   VM421

    ISBN 0—85059–923–7

*Patrick Stephens Limited is part of the
Thorsons Publishing Group,
Wellingborough, Northamptonshire, NN8 2RQ, England*

Printed and bound in Great Britain by
Butler & Tanner Ltd, Frome and London

10 9 8 7 6 5 4 3 2 1

Contents

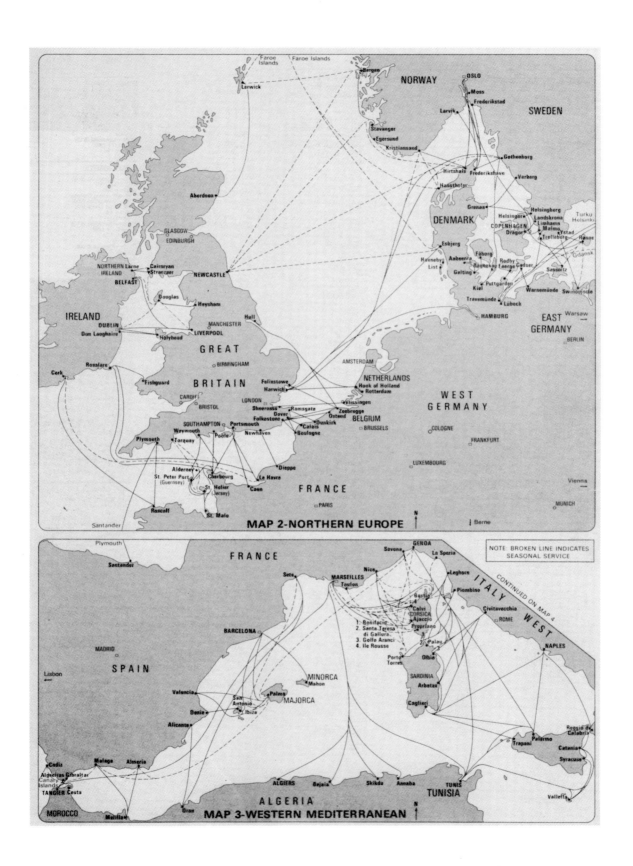

MAP 2-NORTHERN EUROPE

NOTE: BROKEN LINE INDICATES SEASONAL SERVICE

CONTINUED ON MAP 4

MAP 3-WESTERN MEDITERRANEAN

Maps courtesy of *ABC Passenger Shipping Guide.*

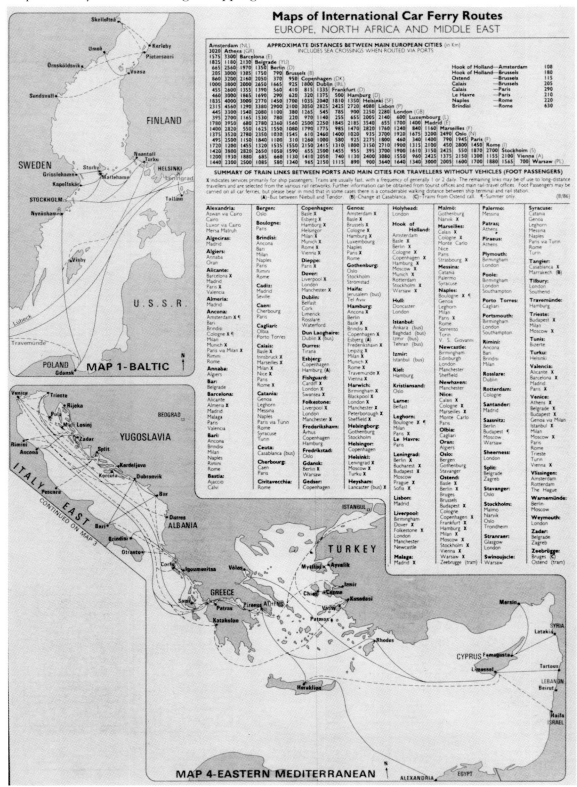

North Sea Ferries' Norsea, *completed in 1987, the largest passenger vessel built in Britain since the* Queen Elizabeth 2 *in 1969* (North Sea Ferries).

Chapter 1

Super-ferries — the evolution

Once the early wide-bodied aircraft became known as 'jumbo jets' it was to be expected that there would quickly be a nautical connotation and soon the first roll-on/roll-off vessels with gross tonnage running into five figures were dubbed 'jumbo ferries'. It was not long before even larger vessels were being hailed as super-ferries and even cruise-ferries. At what precise point a ship becomes worthy of such superlatives has never really been defined and while it has to be acknowledged that size is often relative to routes on which ferries operate, my interpretation is that the super-ferry category really begins at 12,000 tons and therefore mainly embraces ships built since the beginning of the 1970s when there was a sudden and fairly dramatic jump from the 8,000–9,000 ton range that then seemed generally regarded as the ultimate in dimensions.

The incredible growth in ship size for both overnight and short duration crossings has been matched by advances in onboard facilities for passengers and the shore-based technology which has seen ports transformed in the space of two decades with double-width, twin-level loading bridges now accepted as normal on the more intensively–used crossings such as those from Dover across the English Channel or between Sweden and Denmark. Even on the longer routes ferries taking upwards of 1,000 passengers on voyages of ten hours or more are regularly handled in little more time than that allowed for turn-rounds on short-haul routes.

The evolution of the super-ferry began in the earliest days of sea-going vessels with fairly primitive drive-on capability for passengers travelling with their own vehicles — and there is no lack of claimants for the distinction of pioneering the concept on a wider basis than the various river and estuarine ferries that had happily handled wheeled traffic since the days of the horsedrawn cart.

Both the Southern Railway and Townsend Brothers carried crane-loaded cars across the English Channel in the 1930s and garages for a small number of cars that could be driven aboard via special side ramps were included in a trio of train ferries introduced in 1934–5 on the Dover-Dunkirk route, although the vehicle element was very much a secondary consideration. It was the Belgians who were first to appreciate the potential when converting the old steamer *Ville de Liege*, built in 1914, to run as the car ferry *London-Istanbul*. It took 200 passengers with 100 cars loaded over the starboard side where there were no fewer than four ramps at different levels to cope with the tidal range and which were lowered on to the existing quays at Ostend or Dover. The *London-Istanbul* returned to service in 1946 after the Second World War and was scrapped in 1949 following completion of the purpose-built car ferry *Princesse Josephine Charlotte*.

The first true British cross-Channel drive-on ferry was delivered by Wm Denny & Bros of Dumbarton in 1939 for the London, Midland and Scottish Railway and placed on the Stranraer to Larne route as *Princess Victoria*. It had vehicle access via the type of stern entrance then seen only in whale factory ships but also unusual at that time was the choice of Sulzer

Car ferry scene at Dover in the early 1930s with the Townsend Brothers vessel Forde *being unloaded after arriving from Calais. This converted Royal Navy minesweeper continued in service until 1950 and was the forerunner of the Townsend Thoresen fleet's huge modern vessels. Although drive-on/drive-off facilities did not arrive until after* Forde *had been replaced by another former warship, it is interesting to see that a primitive form of stern ramp was provided* (Townsend Thoresen archives).

diesels in preference to steam turbines. The ship became a war loss when mined in May 1940 after a career of only thirteen months but a new *Princess Victoria* of similar design was built by Denny's in 1947 and its sinking with the loss of 128 lives in January 1953 when seas broke through the stern door, was recalled again some 34 years later after the *Herald of Free Enterprise* capsized off Zeebrugge in March 1987 with an even larger number of fatalities.

Further afield there were other, earlier, car ferries. Among them was the wooden-hulled *Motor Princess* built in 1923 for the Canadian Pacific Railway to take 45 drive-on vehicles over the short run from Bellingham to Vancouver Island; the Danish *Heimdal* of 1930 designed to supplement the train ferries of the Great Belt crossing; and two ships both running into Frederikshavn, the *Kronprinsessan Ingrid* (1936) on the route to Gothenburg in Sweden and *Peter Wessel*, with bow and stern doors, used to open a link with Larvik, Norway, a year later.

Ships in which the carriage of cars was the prime factor were still in a minority on British routes and not until 1952 did the British Transport Commission introduce *Lord Warden* as the first true new car ferry for French services from Dover, although even this was still more of a passenger ship with accommodation for 1,500 and just 100 vehicles. Further stern loaders followed, including the imposing *Maid of Kent*, completed seven years later and notable for starting a design trend towards an ability to handle more vehicles and a lower number of passengers. Similar steam-powered vessels were still being built well into the 1960s for British Rail's shipping arm which, by then, had adopted the now familiar Sealink brand name.

Many early car ferries designed for British routes were basically passenger ships with car carrying capacity but then the emphasis began to switch to wheeled traffic and in Maid of Kent, *completed for cross-Channel services from Dover in 1959, there was space for 180 cars and 1,000 passengers, the latter figure being 400 or 500 fewer than in 'classic' ships of the period. Publicized when new as a 'mini liner',* Maid of Kent *set the pattern for Sealink ferry construction and well into the 1960s steam-powered stern loaders were still being built.* Maid of Kent, *always a very popular ship, was broken-up in Spain in 1981 after spending its final years on a seasonal route between Weymouth and Cherbourg (Author).*

Townsend Brothers produced a considerably more modern first new building with *Free Enterprise* in 1962 and after the Townsend family lost control to Nott Industries, later to become European Ferries, a major expansion programme began. Every subsequent new building was equipped with both bow and stern doors for drive-through operation. The company, adopting the Townsend Thoresen marketing name in 1968, managed to stay one jump ahead of the opposition provided by Sealink and its French partners and although both concerns started the 1980s with the Dover-Calais run's largest twin-deck ferries, the ships of the Townsend 'Spirit' class had greater speed, at least until 1987 when they were themselves eclipsed by the 26,000 ton *Pride of Dover* and *Pride of Calais*, the first units of true super-ferry proportions on the Straits of Dover.

Although most jumbos have been introduced for overnight services, the Townsend Thoresen giants, now sailing under the banner of P&O

Free Enterprise, the first purpose built car ferry for Townsend Brothers, appeared in 1962 and presented a contrast in style to the predominantly steam-powered rival fleet of British Railways and its French associate SNCF. It had a light green hull and twin red and black funnels and while only a stern loader, all the subsequent tonnage for the Townsend routes to Calais or Zeebrugge (from 1965) had bow and stern doors. The Dutch-built vessel was sold at the end of 1979 and is still trading in the Eastern Mediterranean as Kimolos *(Alex Duncan).*

European Ferries, are by no means unique in offering huge capacity on shorter crossings. Sweden's Stena Line and Danish State Railways each have vessels close to the 20,000 ton range on services of three to four hours duration and, on the four-hour Canadian east coast route from North Sydney in Nova Scotia to Newfoundland, CN Marine commissioned the 27,213 ton *Caribou* in 1986 — although this ship is an exception to the rule in North America where most of the tonnage on genuine ferry services is still quite small. Some larger former ferries are used on what are actually exclusively cruise services.

The dawn of the ro-ro era enabled short sea operators to make more efficient use of tonnage and the effects were just as far reaching on the longer overnight services which had long been notoriously inefficient in ship utilization. Until the North Sea's first drive-on ferry, *England*, in 1964, many of the vessels employed on runs of half a day's duration or over often spent more hours in port than at sea with loading or discharge of conventional cargo by crane — including what vehicles were available for passage — accounting for a lot of the time. When *England* appeared on the DFDS service between Harwich and Esbjerg and the same company placed the broadly similar twins *Prinsesse Margrethe* and *Kong Olav V* on the Copenhagen-Oslo service two years later, the lack of ramps was overcome by installing side doors from which the ships' own bridges were lowered to the quay. But progress on the North Sea, at least, was sufficiently rapid for *England*'s near sister *Winston Churchill*, completed in 1967, to have bow and stern doors. Indeed the growth in the demand for accompanied cars on routes to Northern Europe and Scandinavia was such that a succession of ferries, all above 8,000 tons, were introduced.

The first British company to go above 10,000 tons was P&O whose Southern Ferries subsidiary went to French builders for the *Eagle* completed in 1971 and used her to start a new service from Southampton to ports in Spain,

Portugal and North Africa. The venture was not a success, with passenger figures never reaching projected levels and the ship, one of a trio of similar design, went to the Mediterranean for cruising. A more rewarding P&O investment was the formation with Dutch partners, Nedlloyd, of North Sea Ferries who produced the first British flag super-ferry *Norland* in 1974 with Dutch sister *Norstar* arriving a year later.

Now North Sea Ferries are operating *Norsea*, delivered in May 1987 and the largest passenger ship built in a British yard for almost twenty years, and a Japanese-built sister *Norsun*. Easily the North Sea's largest ferries at over 30,000 tons, they are still smaller than a number of vessels running in the Baltic, the place at the heart of the super-ferry revolution since the early 1980s — yet an area where drive-on services were not started at all until the late 1950s.

The majority of the really large vessels at present in service have been completed since July 1982 when standards set by the International Convention on Tonnage Measurement of Merchant Ships came into force. The gross tonnage figure is still obtained by dividing the capacity in cubic feet of space within the hull by 100 but additions to the actual areas measured have tended to increase the tonnage figure by as much as two thirds. Spaces within the hull and enclosed areas above deck available for passengers, crew, cargo and stores are again included but fuel tanks are among other extra spaces now measured.

The International Chamber of Shipping has estimated that the tonnage ratio between vessels laid down since 1982 and all the existing ships measured under the previous convention dating from 1969, is in the order of 1.87. This helps to explain the quite dramatic leap past the 30,000 tons mark for many of the recently completed units which would probably have rated in the 18,000 to 20,000 tons range under the old figures. Throughout '*Super-Ferries*' reference to building dates will provide the clearest indication of which gross tonnage rules apply to any particular vessel. All pre-1982 ships undergoing conversion have to be remeasured but remaining ro-ro's can retain the old measurements until July 1992.

One of the clearest indications of the difference in gross tonnage for vessels of similar size in length and capacity, but commissioned before and after 1982, is provided by the two sets of Silja Line twins running across the Baltic between Sweden and Finland from Stockholm. The *Silvia Regina* and *Finlandia*, on the Helsinki run, came into service under the old measurements while *Svea* and *Wellamo*, more recently placed on the Turku route, are subject to the new form of calculation.

	Finlandia and *Silvia Regina*	*Svea* and *Wellamo*
Year	1981–2	1985–6
Gross tonnage	25,905	33,380
Length	166.1 metres	168.0 metres
Width	28.4 metres	27.6 metres
Passengers	2,000	2,000
Overnight berths	1,666	1,800
Vehicles	450 cars	400 cars
Lane metres	1,044	1,803

There have also been dramatic jumps in the tonnage of ferries subject to re-measurement after being rebuilt. Four Townsend Thoresen units given additional vehicle decks in 1985–6 actually emerged with gross tonnage figures doubled. The same company's two former trailer ferries from the 'Stena Searunner' series, which measured 5,700 tons when completed in South Korea, now rate 18,732 tons under the new system following the addition of two decks of passenger accommodation.

With twenty ferries in excess of 30,000 tons already operating or in the course of construction it is fascinating to speculate to what size the ships of the next decade will go. In construction terms there appears to be no limitation but the obvious controlling influence is one of availability, both in terms of passengers/vehicles and in the existence of port facilities. The Baltic routes can support ships with space for 2,000 passengers on a year-round basis at present yet six more are currently on order and it will be interesting to see whether by the early 1990s rivals Viking Line and Silja Line will actually be able to fill their awesome giants.

Servicing such huge units is also a problem and it is difficult to visualize just how much further operators can go beyond present levels on overnight services without having to drastically extend turn-around times, a course of action that would defeat the whole ferry concept.

Six decades of ferry development

Year	Vessel	GRT	Pass	Cars	Rail metres
1923	*Motor Princess*	1,243	500	40	–
1930	*Heimdal*	1,083	400	60	–
1934	**Twickenham Ferry*	2,839	500	25	12 pass coaches
1936	*Kronpr. Ingrid*	987	600	40	–
1937	*Peter Wessel*	1,956	600	70	–
1939	*Princess Victoria*	2,197	1,000	40	–
1947	*Princess Victoria*	2,694	1,500	40	–
1949	*Pr. J. Charlotte*	2,572	750	100	–
1952	*Lord Warden*	3,333	1,500	120	–
1954	**Kong Frederik IX*	4,084	1,500	115	258
1957	**Theodor Huess*	5,583	1,500	220	300
1959	*Maid of Kent*	3,920	1,000	180	–
	Napoleon	5,564	1,200	100	–
	*Sassnitz	6,164	1,017	40	379
1964	*England*	8,221	688	100	–
1966	*Svea*	8,554	784	215	–
	Prins Hamlet	8,688	1,000	165	–
	Jupiter/Venus	9,499	600	180	–
1971	*Eagle*	11,609	800	259	–
1972	*Sun Rise*	12,104	1,418	210	–
	†Med. Sea	16,384	854	350	–
1973	*Sun Flower 8*	12,572	1,079	78	+ 84 lorries
1974	*Peter Pan*	12,528	1,800	470	–
	Svea Corona	12,578	1,200	240	–
	Dana Regina	12,960	1,006	260	–
	Norland	12,988	1,243	520	–
	Sun Flower II	13,614	1,206	192	–
1975	*Tor Britannia*	15,656	1,507	490	–
1976	*Tor Scandinavia*	15,673	1,507	440	–
1977	*Finnjet*	24,065	1,790	374	–
1981	*Silvia Regina*	25,905	2,000	450	–
1985	*Svea*	33,830	2,000	400	–
	Mariella	37,799	2,500	580	–

*Train Ferries   † Conversion from cargo vessel.

Below *Completed in 1964,* England *combined the style and elegant lines of a traditional passenger ship with vehicle carrying capacity and was the North Sea's earliest drive-on ferry when placed by DFDS on the Esbjerg–Harwich route. The outline of the forward side door can clearly by seen in this view of the vessel in the River Tyne in 1981, towards the end of its DFDS career. A year later* England *was bought by Cunard Line and spent eighteen months on a Cape Town–Port Stanley service while the Falklands airport was under construction, thereafter being laid-up at Birkenhead apart from brief spells of troop carrying duties in connection with military exercises. Late in 1986* England *was bought by Greek interests and left for the Red Sea under the name* America XIII, *flying the Panamanian flag. Eventual cruising use is likley — a return to a winter role of the late 1960s when* England *visited the Caribbean in successive years (Author).*

Super-ferries:
The top 50 vessels in service or under construction

No.	Vessel	GRT	Owner	Pass	Cars	Flag
1	*New Building*	50,000*	EFFOA	2,500	450	Finland
2	*New Building*	50,000*	Johnson Line	2,500	450	Sweden
3	*Mariella*	37,799*	SF Line	2,500	580	Finland
4	*Olympia*	37,583*	Red. Slite	2,500	580	Sweden
5	*New Building (1)*	35,000*	Red. Slite	2,200	650	Sweden
6	*New Building (2)*	35,000*	Red. Slite	2,200	650	Sweden
7	*New Building (1)*	35,000*	Olau Line	1,800	500	Germany
8	*New Building (2)*	35,000*	Olau Line	1,800	500	Germany
9	*Svea*	33,830*	Johnson Line	2,000	400	Sweden
10	*Wellamo*	33,818*	EFFOA	2,000	400	Finland
11	*Amorella*	33,000*	SF Line	2,200	640	Finland
12	*New Building (2)*	33,000*	SF Line	2,200	640	Finland
13	*Norsea*	31,727*	P&O	1,258	850	Britain
14	*Norsun*	31,727*	Nedlloyd	1,258	850	Holland
15	*Peter Pan*	31,360*	TT Line	1,600	550	Germany
16	*Nils Holgersson*	31,360*	Wallenius	1,600	550	Sweden
17	*Koningin Beatrix*	31,189*	SMZ	2,100	485	Holland
18	*Kronprins Harald*	31,122*	Jahre	1,432	750	Norway
19	*Stena Germanica*	30,244*	Stena Line	2,500	700	Sweden
20	*Stn. Scandinavica*	30,244*	Stena Line	2,500	700	Sweden
21	*Caribou*	27,213*	Mar. Atlantic	1,342	350	Canada
22	*Norland*	27,200*	P&O	900	550	Britain
23	*Norstar*	27,200*	Nedlloyd	900	550	Holland
24	*Ile de Beaute*	27,000*	SNCM	2,300	800	France
25	*Stardancer*	26,748*	Sundance	1,606	520	Bahamas
26	*Pride of Dover*	26,000*	P&O Euro F.	2,300	650	Britain
27	*Pride of Calais*	26,000*	P&O Euro F.	2,300	650	Britain
28	*Silvia Regina*	25,905	Johnson Line	2,000	450	Sweden
29	*Finlandia*	25,678	EFFOA	2,000	450	Finland
30	*Finnjet*	24,065	Silja/Finnjet	1,790	374	Finland
31	*Bretagne*	22,500*	Brittany F.	2,000	600	France
32	*Birka Princess*	21,484*	Birka Line	1,100	88	Finland
33	*Peder Paars*	19,763*	DSB	2,000	331	Denmark
34	*Niels Klim*	19,763*	DSB	2,000	331	Denmark
35	*Baltic Ferry*	18,732*	European F.	650	570	Britain
36	*Nordic Ferry*	18,732*	European F.	650	570	Britain
37	*Graip*	18,700*	Norstrom & Thulin	1,700	600	Sweden
38	*New Hamanasu*	17,261*	Shin Nihonkai	920	400	Japan
39	*New Shirayuri*	17,261*	Shin Nihonkai	920	400	Japan
40	*Kpr. Victoria*	17,062	Stena Line	2,100	500	Sweden
41	*St. Nicholas*	17,043	British Fer.	2,100	480	British
42	*Stena Danica*	16,494	Stena Line	2,300	600	Sweden
43	*Stena Jutlandica*	16,494	Stena Line	2,300	600	Sweden
44	*Mediterranean Sea*	16,384	Karageorgis	854	345	Cyprus
45	*Pr. Ragnhild*	16,332	Jahre Line	896	600	Norway
46	*Tor Scandinavia*	15,673	DFDS	1,507	490	Denmark
47	*Tor Britannia*	15,656	DFDS	1,507	490	Denmark
48	*Viking Sally*	15,576	Red. Sally	2,000	460	Finland
49	*Oari Maru*	15,139*	Nihon Enkai	656	400	Japan
50	*Mediterranean Sky*	14,941	Karageorgis	800	300	Greece

(*Measured under 1982 gross tonnage rules)

Chapter 2

Super-ferries from Britain

The majority of British ferry operators found medium-sized tonnage adequate for their needs and for a decade until the reconstructions and new buildings of the last two or three years the only 'jumbo' flying the Red Ensign and purpose-built for the route it served was North Sea Ferries' *Norland*. Sealink's entry into the big ship league in 1983 with *St. Nicholas* was through the charter market and the new *Norsea* and Dover-based twins *Pride of Dover* and *Pride of Calais* apart, all other ferries of over 12,000 tons which regularly visit British ports are from the fleets of foreign operators. They will be joined in 1989 by Brittany Ferries who move into the big ship league for the first time with a 22,500 ton new building. Olau Line also have two giants on order.

North Sea Ferries

The established concept of sea connections for passengers and vehicles via the shortest routes from affluent Southern England to the Continent was shattered from 1965 when P&O and the Dutch group Nedlloyd jointly formed North Sea Ferries and opened a gateway from England's northern industrial heartland to Europe, starting a two ship service between Hull and Rotterdam's Europoort.

Substantial wheeled freight space for both lorries and unaccompanied trailers was provided in an overnight service inaugurated on 17 December 1965 by the 3,450 ton British flag *Norwave* which was joined the following March by Dutch-registered sister, *Norwind*. The partnership proved highly successful and

in 1974 the near 13,000 ton *Norland* and *Norstar* took over with the original pair switched to a new route between Hull and Zeebrugge in Belgium.

While the earlier ferries were equipped with bow and stern doors, their successors on the Europoort run have only stern access. This feature was repeated in the design of a pair of outstanding new ships ordered in May 1985 and delivered two years later with both the British flag *Norsea* and its Japanese-built sister *Norsun* commissioned in May 1987, at which point *Norland* and *Norstar* were sent back to the Bremerhaven yard of builders Seebeckwerft, to be lengthened before switching to the Belgian route.

Norland/Norstar

Owner P&O Ferries/Nedlloyd. **Flag** British/Dutch. **Operator** North Sea Ferries. **Route** Hull-Zeebrugge. **Built** AG Weser, Bremerhaven, 1974; lengthened by builders, 1987. **Gross tonnage** 27,000 (12,502 before conversion). **Net tonnage** not available (7,403 before conversion.) **Length** 173 m. **Width** 24.7m. **Draught** 5.5 m. **Machinery** 2 SWD diesels of 13,240 hp. **Speed** 19 knots. **Passengers** 900. **Cabin berths** 900. **Vehicle capacity** 520 cars. **Vehicle access** Stern.

The North Sea Ferries partners had their first ships built by A.G. Weser and went back to the German yard, now trading as Seebeckwerft, for *Norland* and *Norstar*, vessels which marked the beginning of an important and distinctive sequence of passenger ferries from Bremerhaven including Olau Line's *Olau*

Hollandia and *Olau Britannia* in 1981–2 and, more recently, the *Peter Pan* and *Nils Holgersson* for TT Line. In many respects *Norwave* and *Norwind* were really ro-ro freight ferries accommodating only about 250 passengers but for their replacements NSF put equal emphasis on the passenger element and produced ships with space for 1,243 passengers and cabin space for over 1,000 of them.

Two full-length vehicle decks with an upper platform for further cars could handle 90 trailers and 250 cars on a total of 1,570 running metres of space, but access was by way of the stern only with drive-through facilities considered unnecessary for ships planned to run on a balanced and economical 14/15 hour schedule which allowed plenty of time in port for handling of freight, including up to 50 export cars carried in a separate hold. Another important factor that also had to be taken into consideration was the time-consuming but unavoidable ritual of locking in and out King George Dock to reach Hull terminal which made greater acceleration completely pointless.

A unique NSF feature surviving from the early days is the inclusion of dinner and full English breakfast in passage fares. Meals aboard *Norland* and *Norstar* are served in a huge 500-seat cafeteria. Other main public areas include the 440-seat Continental Lounge plus

Norstar *outward bound from Hull in June 1982 while sister ship* Norland *was in the South Atlantic. The two vessels ran with plain black hulls until the company name was added in 1980* (Author).

smaller bars and lounges. *Norland*'s maiden departure from Hull took place on 10 June 1974 and sister *Norstar*, launched a month later, was completed in time to join the service with a first crossing from Holland on 20 December. Both routes attracted steadily increasing business but there was a period of major disruption from April 1982 when *Norland* was requisitioned by the British Ministry of Defence to carry troops to the South Atlantic following the invasion of the Falkland Islands by Argentina.

Taken-over after discharging passengers and freight at Hull on 17 April, *Norland* sailed south just nine days later carrying the 2nd Batallion Parachute Regiment and with helicopter pads fitted forward of the funnel and at the stern. Additional fuel and fresh water capacity was provided together with equipment for replenishment at sea, and 25 days out of Portsmouth *Norland* was to be found in San Carlos Water following the landings. The ferry later left to rendezvous at sea with *Canberra* and also went to South Georgia to meet up with *Queen Elizabeth 2* but returned on four further occasions to the notorious San Carlos 'Bomb Alley'. Later there were separate sailings to Montevideo and Puerto Madryn in Argentina for the repatriation of prisoners and then *Norland* took Parachute Regiment survivors to Ascension Island on the first stage of their journey home. *Norland*'s contribution was not over and the Department of Trade refused to release the ship which, from July 1982, began shuttling between Ascension and Port Stanley with men, military stores and supplies in a role

Norland *in the thick of the Falklands action in San Carlos Water on 24 May 1982 with HMS* Antelope *sinking astern after an attack by Argentine aircraft* (Ministry of Defence).

which continued into 1983, *Norland* finally arriving back in Hull on 1 February after steaming a total of 65,000 miles and with a crowd estimated at over 5,000 lining the dockside to give a rousing welcome.

During her sister's long absence *Norstar* continued to operate. NSF used Rederi Sally's *Viking 6* at first as a chartered stand-in for *Norland* before the rather larger *Saint Patrick II* was brought in from ICL. *Norland* made a short passage across the Humber to Immingham after her return for a major mechanical overhaul and internal refurbishment and resumed services to Rotterdam on Tuesday 19 April.

The drama was not over for the Falklands veteran, however, and when forced to make an emergency course change to avoid a cargo vessel while leaving Europoort in June 1985, a stabilizer fin touched bottom and ripped a 15-ft gash in the shell plating. With the engine room flooding *Norland* began settling at the stern and developed a list but was towed to an ore terminal and over 600 passengers were taken off with the help of ladders. Repairs by a Dutch yard took more than three months and with no

suitable replacement available an alternate night sailing pattern was maintained by *Norstar*.

During 1985 *Norland* and *Norstar* were improved internally with the cafeterias fully carpeted and new servery equipment installed to increase the variety of hot dishes available. All the special and standard grade cabins were carpeted and, for the first time, provided with individual keys. By then both new ships for the Rotterdam route were under construction and, as expected, it was confirmed that the existing sisters would switch to the Zeebrugge service which had expanded to such an extent in the area of wheeled freight that two chartered trailer ferries were needed to sail in parallel with *Norwind* and *Norwave*.

Then, as part of a £90 million investment also including the new tonnage, NSF announced that prior to transferring to the Belgian run, *Norland* and *Norstar* would be sent in turn to builders Seebeckwerft at Bremerhaven to be lengthened by 20.25 metres. The operation involved each hull being cut vertically amidships to allow insertion of a new mid-body in an operation taking no more than seven weeks for each vessel, thanks mainly to the yard's knowledge of the ships and its ability to pre-construct the new sections. *Norland* was first to go immediately after the new *Norsea* was

commissioned and emerged to begin Zeebrugge sailings during July. *Norstar's* debut came a little later and both ships appeared in NSF's new two-tone blue colour scheme devised for the Dutch route ships.

The additional centre section boosts trailer space by 45 12 metre units and provides enhanced cabin accommodation on the upper deck. Passenger capacity overall is reduced to 900 berths with all standard cabins beneath the car deck removed to allow enlargement of the former export car space into a fully fledged cellular hold. In this form *Norland* and *Norstar* offer greater capacity than the four ships previously employed to Zeebrugge. A new terminal in the outer harbour of this port was opened in 1985 replacing a previous berth through the lock in Prins Filipsdok.

The designed service speed of around 18 knots from a pair of Stork/Werkspoor TM410 engines is still maintained despite the extra length and while 18.00 is still the Hull departure time for both Rotterdam and Zeebrugge sailings, the long established practice of the Belgian service ship locking out first has been maintained. In-bound arrival for each route is also the same at 08.00 and usually the sailing from Rotterdam is first to berth. The new Hull Terminal, provided by Associated British Ports and the third to stand on the site was officially opened by Princess Margaret and is named in her honour.

Below *More drama for* Norland*! After being holed when taking action to avoid a collision near the Hook of Holland on 7 June 1985 the engine room flooded and the listing, disabled vessel is seen being moved back to Europoort (with lifeboats swung out) to safely disembark over 600 passengers* (J. Terol).

Left Norland *in the Seebeckwerft dry dock with the new mid-body section having been floated into place and with the original bow section in the process of being returned* (Seebeckwerft).

Below left *Work on* Norland *and* Norstar *progressed simultaneously during May and June and lengthening of the two ships was completed on schedule and in just 49 working days. Here* Norstar's *new section is in position prior to the floating dock being raised for the massive welding operation to make three separate portions into a single unit* (Seebeckwerft).

Above Norland *re-entered service on the Zeebrugge route on 1 July 1987 and is seen at Hull after an early arrival from the Belgian port. Now measured at 27,000 tons,* Norland *and* Norstar *are only slightly smaller than their newly built replacements on the Rotterdam run and have been brought up to the same standards of internal comfort* (Author).

Below Norland *looking particularly impressive when pictured from the air shortly after leaving Zeebrugge for Hull* (Henderyckz – Izegem).

Left Norsea *on its way down the Govan slipway and into the River Clyde following launching by Queen Elizabeth, the Queen Mother, in September 1986* (North Sea Ferries).

Norsea/Norsun

Owner P&O Ferries/Nedlloyd. **Flag** British/Dutch. **Operator** North Sea Ferries. **Route** Hull-Rotterdam Europoort. **Built** Govan Shipbuilders 1987/Nippon Kokan KK, Japan, in 1987. **Gross tonnage** 31,727. **Net tonnage** 16,000. **Length** 179 m. **Width** 25.4m. **Draught** 6.1 m. **Machinery** 4 Sulzer diesels of 18,390 hp. **Speed** 18.5 knots. **Passengers** 1,258. **Cabin berths** 1,224. **Vehicle capacity** 850 cars. **Vehicle access** Stern.

North Sea Ferries ended months of speculation early in 1985 with the official announcement of an order for what they termed a 'cruise ferry' for the Hull-Rotterdam Europoort service. Govan Shipbuilders beat off strong European and Scandinavian competition to secure the contract from P&O while their Dutch partners Nedlloyd looked set to order an identical sister ship from Van der Gissen-de Noord, then at an advanced stage with construction of the Zeeland Steamship Company's Hook of Holland-Harwich ferry *Koningin Beatrix* on their huge covered slipway at Krimpen an den Ijssel, near Rotterdam.

However, with no support from the Dutch government forthcoming Van der Gissen were forced to withdraw and Nedlloyd looked instead to Japan and put their order in the hands of Nippon Kokan KK of Tsurumi.

The largest passenger vessel built in Britain since the *Queen Elizabeth 2* was completed for Cunard just four miles down the River Clyde in 1969. NSF's third generation giant was given a royal send-off when launched as *Norsea* by Queen Elizabeth, the Queen Mother, on 9 September 1986. Despite their late start the Kokan yard made up for lost time and launched the Dutch running mate without ceremony as *Norsun* even earlier.

The main design objective was to achieve extra freight space within the size limitations imposed by the lock giving access to the Humber from Hull's King George Dock system and in view of the fairly relaxed turn-around margins additional capacity was created by the incorporation of a cellular hold at tank top level for-

Below Norsea *in its Beneluxhaven berth when visiting Rotterdam's Europoort on 11 May, just two days after making a belated maiden voyage. Bad weather disruption to final trials on the Clyde was blamed by Govan Shipbuilders for delivery a month late* (Author).

The new berth in Hull's King George Dock, provided for North Sea Ferries by Associated British Ports along with a spacious new terminal building, with Norsea loading cars for Rotterdam (Author).

ward of the engine room. In all 2,250 lane metres is available for about 180 trailers or 850 cars — double that in *Norland* and *Norstar* as built, but giving a similar passenger total of 1,250.

There are 1,124 berths in a total of 446 cabins situated forward on three different decks, reflecting the modern trend of isolating sleeping areas from the bustle and noise of public rooms and also engine spaces. All the cabins were constructed in Govan Shipbuilders' own cabin module facility and wheeled aboard complete in need only of fixing to the deck and the connection of main services. Meals are still included in ticket prices and the cafeteria is in two parts with a forward area seating 464 and an after room for 246.

Because of the one hour difference between British and Dutch time, varying service speeds are needed to maintain schedules and a mix of two nine-cylinder and two six-cylinder engines of Swiss Sulzer design, built under licence by Wartsila of Finland, have been provided. Crossing westbound from Rotterdam, the two larger 87 ton units are normally used for a speed of 16.5 knots with one of the six-cylinder engines available to provide back-up as required. Travelling from Hull, *Norsea* and *Norsun* need to maintain 18.5 knots from three engines while the other 64 ton six-cylinder engine is in reserve in the event of bad weather.

Speed requirements apart, consideration also had to be given to the fact that every sailing involves traversing relatively shallow water, and voyage data from *Norland* and *Norstar* was given close scrutiny to ensure selection of the best power margin. The need to support additional deadweight resulting from the cellular hold resulted in an unusually full hull for a passenger ship, and for fuel efficiency the largest possible propellers of a Kamewa controllable pitch design were selected.

Considerable shore work was undertaken in Hull before the large ships entered service. In addition to a new berth, NSF opened a unified terminal and administrative headquarters in place of the former office block located well away from separate terminal facilities for motorists and foot passengers. The existing ramp in the Europoort's Beneluxhavn has been retained but as *Norsea* and *Norsun* are some 25 metres longer than their immediate predecessors (as built), the harbour edge was sheet piled to enable a greater depth of water to be provided.

Above *An impressive aerial view of* Norsun *which entered service from Rotterdam on 12 May just four days after* Norsea's *first crossing. The Japanese-built giant carried over 800 new Nissan cars on its delivery voyage to Holland and then spent several days showing the flag in Rotterdam before a commercial debut* (North Sea Ferries).

Right Norsun *dressed overall while open to the public in Rotterdam prior to moving to Europoort for the maiden sailing to Hull* (Author).

The arrival of the new tonnage and its striking white and two tone blue livery in place of the rather conservative black hulls and orange and black funnels of the previous two decades, has also seen NSF's traditional low key approach swept aside by a fresh and aggressive publicity and marketing aimed with some success at increasing both passenger business and expanding in the freight sphere.

P&O European Ferries

Early in 1987 the P&O Group made a successful takeover bid for European Ferries, one of the world's largest independent ferry companies with five wholly-owned ship-owning or operating subsidiaries using modern tonnage on eight routes from mainland Britain to Holland, Belgium, France and Northern Ireland. This marked something of a reversal in ferry fortunes as European Ferries had acquired P&O's own English Channel ferry operation as recently as the beginning of 1985 but, two years later, after the slump in world oil prices had adversely affected substantial property investments in the United States, the European Ferries shareholders were recommended by their directors to accept the P&O offer which valued the company, also owners and operators of the ports of Felixstowe and Larne, at £300 million.

Known to the travelling public through the trading name of Townsend Thoresen, the activities continued with immediate adoption of the P&O houseflag the first outward sign of change. All ships in the fleet received P&O's pale blue funnel colours during April and then, from October 1987, the Townsend Thoresen brand name was dropped in favour of P&O European Ferries. From this point the dark blue P&O colour scheme was progressively applied to the hulls of vessels as they went in turn for annual overhaul. In June, the company accepted delivery of the first of its most significant ferries to date, the 26,000 ton *Pride of Dover* which was joined by sister-ship *Pride of Calais* before the end of the year. These ships marked the end of a development programme costing more than £100 million and including extensive rebuilding of existing vessels during 1985 and 1986.

European Ferries previously ran its services through three subsidiaries: Dover to Calais, Boulogne and Zeebrugge by Townsend Car Ferries (acquired 1957); Portsmouth to Cherbourg and Le Havre by Thoresen Car Ferries (acquired 1968); and Felixstowe to Zeebrugge and Rotterdam, and Cairnryan to Larne, by Atlantic Steam Navigation Company (acquired in 1971) and trading as Transport Ferry Service.

From 22nd October 1987 these operating companies were simplified to P&O Ferries (Dover), P&O Ferries (Portsmouth) and P&O Ferries (Felixstowe). Also part of efforts to establish a new corporate image was a decision to drop all reference to the former Townsend 'Free Enterprise' slogan and all vessels named in this style were re-christened. However, ownership of all the various units in the fleet remains in the name of the original companies and other holding companies such as Monarch Steamship Company and Stanhope Shipping.

Since the early 1980s annual passenger carryings have considerably exceeded the three million mark—a remarkable advance when it is remembered that as late as 1957 the original Townsend company was still running out of Dover with a converted Second World War frigate often making only one round trip a day. The real expansion did not start until the middle of the 1960s.

The Townsend name soon became synonymous with the car ferry concept but the family were ship owners long before the start of the first cross-Channel service between Dover and Calais using a chartered coaster in 1928. Retired Army Captain, Stuart Townsend, was the driving force behind the venture. Competition with the long-established services of the Southern Railway intensified from 1930 when Townsend began using the *Forde*, rebuilt from a minesweeper bought off shipbreakers for £5,000. Townsend saw the great advantage of vehicles being driven directly on to the decks of ferries by means of bridges and his company looked in 1939 at the Norwegian vessel *Peter Wessel* which had both stern and bow doors but the imminence of the Second World War, among other factors, prevented a purchase.

Townsends re-opened their service in 1947 and replaced the old *Forde* with another warship conversion in 1950. A year later drive-on/drive-off facilities came to the Dover-Calais route due largely to the initiative of the Townsend company which found a surplus Callender Hamilton military bridge and moved it to Calais for installation at the Quai Maritime. At this time the service was still being run by a private company but in 1956 it became necessary to go public and Stuart Townsend lost both the office of chairman and overall control, Nott Industries taking over from the beginning of 1957.

A new building programme produced purpose-built tonnage and enabled a Dover-Zeebrugge link to be started in 1965. Two years later, Nott Industries purchased the entire share capital of Thoresen Car Ferries A/S, a Norwegian company which had build up a successful four-ship fleet serving Cherbourg and Le Havre from Southampton. It was announced that the two companies would be known as European Ferries and although both continued to trade under their original names, moves towards integration began in 1969 with the adoption of the Townsend Thoresen title. There was further expansion at the end of 1971 when the Atlantic Steam Navigation Company, trading as Transport Ferry Service with seven modern stern loaders on ro-ro freight routes from Preston across the Irish Sea and between Felixstowe and Europe, was bought from the state-owned National Freight Corporation.

The mid-1970s brought new routes and tonnage including four identical Danish-built passenger ships with cabin accommodation for longer runs from Felixstowe to Zeebrugge and from Southampton to France. Then orders were placed in Germany for three new generation vessels of almost 8,000 tons and taking up to 1,300 passengers and 350 cars on twin-level vehicle decks between Dover and Calais and capable of being turned round between crossings in as little as 45 minutes.

With sufficient speed to complete one more full round trip in each 24 hour period than ships of main rivals Sealink and its French partner SNCF, these units helped Townsend Thoresen to maintain their edge in a fiercely competitive market. The company replied to the approval of a fixed link Channel Tunnel connection from Britain to France with orders for *Pride of Dover* and *Pride of Calais*, the largest short route car ferries seen so far.

Further additional capacity, especially for freight, was achieved at a fraction of the cost of new tonnage by lifting four vessels right into the 'super–ferry' category. The quartet, two of the Danish-built ships from 1975 and a pair of older units from a series built in Holland for service from Dover, were rebuilt in Bremerhaven with the superstructure raised to allow construction of new full-length upper vehicle decks and new bow sections. In an equally intriguing operation during the same period of time, two trailer ferries were converted to provide high quality accommodation for 650 passengers thus allowing the deployment of larger capacity tonnage to South Coast routes.

While Townsend Thoresen joined other operators and Kent port authorities to form the Flexilink organization in opposition to the Channel Tunnel project and actively promoted the big new ships as potential 'Chunnel Beaters', it will be interesting to see whether the ferry companies are still strongly represented at Dover when the fixed link eventually opens. Townsend Thoresen certainly looked set to battle it out but whether the takeover by P&O will, in the longer term, result in a re-think remains to be seen.

Pride of Sandwich/ Pride of Walmer

Owner European Ferries. **Flag** British. **Operator** P&O European Ferries. **Route** Dover-Zeebrugge. **Built** Werft Gusto, Schiedam, Holland, in 1972/1973; rebuilt Schichau, Unterweser, Bremerhaven, 1985/1986. **Gross tonnage** 12,503. **Net tonnage** 5,941. **Length** 139.4 m. **Width** 22 m. **Draught** 5.2 m. **Machinery** 3 Stork-Werkspoor diesels of 9,700/9,820 hp. **Speed** 19.3 knots. **Passengers** 1,035. **Cabin berths** 64. **Vehicle capacity** 370 cars. **Vehicle access** Bow and stern. **Former names:** *Free Enterprise VI* and *VII*.

The first purpose-built Townsend car ferry, completed in 1961, appeared as *Free Enterprise* and began a style of naming that was to extend through almost twenty years of expansion. When a second new building, the first ferry on the Channel deigned for drive-through working with bow and stern doors, came along as *Free Enterprise II* in 1965, the earlier ship had the suffix 'I' added to its name. A year later when the same Schiedam yard completed the larger *Free Enterprise III* the standard Townsend passenger ferry design had evolved with five similar examples put into commission on the Calais and Zeebrugge services from 1969 to 1974.

Although strikingly different in appearance from the much more traditional lines of tonnage operated by Sealink and their French and Belgian associates, the ships of the 'FE' series looked attractive with pale green hulls, white superstructure and black-topped red funnels. They never came over quite as well after 1977 and the adoption of a new livery of orange hulls with a green funnel — but that was nothing to the indignities heaped upon *Free Enterprise VI* and *Free Enterprise VII*. These two vessels were rebuilt in 1985 and 1986 to increase capacity to Zeebrugge in an exercise which left them as clear contenders for the distinction of being among the ugliest ferries afloat!

To be realistic, ferry operators long since ceased worrying about the looks of their vessels: all that matters these days is the ability to handle extra freight and in this respect the conversions can only be hailed as a considerable success. In their original condition *Free Enterprise VI* and *VII* were 117.5 metres long and could carry 250 cars or 21 lorries but now with length increased to 139.4 metres there is space for 320 cars or 60 lorries and accommodation remains for over 1,000 passengers.

Above *The superstructure of* Free Enterprise VI *being lifted off by four crane barges at the Schichau Unterweser Yard in Bremerhaven during 1985. The superstructure was placed in the area of quay at the bottom of the picture and then replaced intact after a new bow section had been fitted and the hull built-up to enclose a complete new upper vehicle deck* (Schichau Unterweser).

The conversions were undertaken by Schichau Unterweser AG at Bremerhaven. The first task was to cut and lift off the entire superstructure by floating crane. This reposed on the quayside while the extra upper deck was built-up and new bow sections added. The latter were produced as a single hull for the two ships and side launched at Leche into the River Geeste. Later this strange hull was separated in dry dock after being moved to the main Schichau construction yard on the banks of the Weser and its two halves added to the *Free Enterprise* sisters.

As built the *VI* and *VII* had a far more advanced internal layout than rival ferries which stuck quite rigidly to the old classic passenger ship style with rows of seats on either beam and main public rooms forward and aft. The Townsend ships enjoyed open plan layouts utilizing the full width of the superstructure. They were even improved in the winter of 1984–5 in earlier visits to Bremerhaven when catering arrangements were changed to feature a spacious new cafeteria while retaining separate small *à la* carte and freight drivers' restaurants. The information desk was re-sited in a central position on the main passenger deck with other improvements to bar and shopping areas and this remained unchanged through the subsequent re-building.

Free Enterprise VI returned to service on 28 October 1985 and was immediately replaced in Bremerhaven by *FE VII* which was itself back in operation by the end of February 1986. No changes were made to the machinery of the two ships during the conversion and performance has not been adversely affected by these changes, three Stork Werkspoor TM410 eight cylinder diesels drive triple screws and achieve a service speed of 19.5 knots. The two ships have continued making two return sailings between Dover and Zeebrugge in each 24-hour period but have each also made occasional appearances at Calais since the alterations.

During the summer of 1987 both vessels carried P&O funnel markings, the 'Townsend Thoresen' name on their hulls being painted out immediately after the October adoption of the P&O name. Then, early in 1988 when they returned from annual overhaul, fully repainted in the new P&O livery, *Free Enterprise VI* became *Pride of Sandwich* and its sister is now sailing as *Pride of Walmer*.

Viking Venturer/Viking Valiant

Owner Thoresen Car Ferries Ltd. **Flag** British. **Operator** P&O European Ferries. **Route** Portsmouth–Le Havre/. **Built** Alborg Vaerft, Denmark, in 1974–1975; Rebuilt Schichau Unterweser, Bremerhaven, 1986. **Gross tonnage** 14,760. **Net tonnage** Not available. **Length** 139.4 m. **Width** 22 m. **Draught** 5.2 m. **Machinery** 3 Stork-Werkspoor diesels of 14,300 hp. **Speed** 21 knots. **Passengers** 1,316. **Cabin berths** 275. **Vehicle capacity** 370 cars. **Vehicle access** Bow and stern.

Two years after taking over the Thoresen ser-

Left and below Free Enterprise VI *before and after re-building in Bremerhaven in 1985. The open doors of the new upper vehicle deck can be seen in the view of the ship as it now operates on the Townsend Thoresen service between Dover and Zeebrugge. There is also a new foremast with an additional pair of forward lifeboats immediately behind* (Author and Townsend Thoresen).

Following the takeover of Townsend Thoresen by P&O at the beginning of 1987, first moves towards a change of corporate image occurred during April when the familiar green Townsend funnel colours were replaced throughout the entire fleet by P&O's light blue complete with house flag. **Free Enterprise VII**, *entering Zeebrugge's inner harbour in June, wears the P&O funnel colours but still has the old-style Townsend logo prominently displayed towards the stern* (Maritime Photographic).

vices from Southampton to France, European Ferries began moves to replace the station's three original Norwegian-flag passenger ferries *Viking I*, *Viking II* and *Viking III* by including a trio of larger replacement vessels in a five-year building programme which also provided further tonnage for the Dover-based services. The 6,387 ton, 1,200 passenger ships were ordered from Denmark's Aalborg Vaerft and even before the first was launched on the opening day of June 1974 as *Viking Venturer*, the class had become known as 'Super Vikings'.

Viking Venturer made a Southampton debut on 22 January 1975 but already company thinking was changing and the second in the series, the October-launched *Viking Valiant*, went directly to the then newly-started Felixstowe-Zeebrugge route in May 1975 and did not go to Southampton until January of the following year when ship number three, *Viking Voyager*, arrived at Felixstowe. By then a fourth unit had been ordered and this was completed as *Viking Viscount* and also went to Felixstowe, entering service in May 1976. It was not until some nine years later, in the sum-

mer of 1985, that all of the quartet were running to Cherbourg and Le Havre. By this date Southampton had been abandoned and all sailings were from Portsmouth.

The triple screw arrangement of the 'Free Enterprise' ships was repeated and again power came from three Stork-Werkspoor medium speed diesels with a nine-cylinder centre unit and two eight-cylinder wing engines producing 14,300 hp and a service speed of over 20 knots. The open plan layout of the Dover ships was also incorporated but because of their design for longer sailings with overnight crossings nearly 300 berths were provided in standard cabins and also upper deck luxury cabins with private facilities. The latter were removed on *Viking Venturer* and *Viking Valiant* prior to summer sailings in 1984 and replaced by Club Class lounges with wide fully-reclining seats with head and foot rests and bar and refreshment services for which supplementary fares were charged.

Although three of Townsend Thoresen's freight ferries were called-up for South Atlantic service during the Falklands War of 1982, the 'Super Vikings' did not have sufficient cabin berths to be seriously considered. However, *Viking Venturer* was chartered by the Ministry of Defence for the opening months of 1983 to go to the Persian Gulf as an exhibition ship for the British arms industry. In this role she departed in January 1983, following overhaul in Le Havre, to travel to the Gulf via the Mediterranean and the Suez Canal. Later in the same year both *Viking Venturer* and *Viking Valiant* broke new ground when visiting

Poole to run return charter sailings to Cherbourg and, on occasions, Townsend Thoresen also used the ships for publicity visits on the French side with Rouen among places to receive calls.

Viking Venturer was first to go to Bremerhaven and arrived at the Schichau yard in December 1985 with work to remove the superstructure commencing early the following month, although this time the operation was rather more complicated than for the *Free Enterprise* ships. A greater amount of passenger accommodation had to be lifted off in two sections with the aft area going first. The new bow section, already launched joined to that intended for *Viking Valiant*, was fitted in dry dock before the hull was built-up to

form the additional vehicle deck and then topped-off with the replacement of the superstructure. The passenger accommodation was not affected by the 'jumboization' process apart from the provision of a new restaurant for freight drivers and additional lounge seating forward. Like the 'FE' ships, both the 'Super Vikings' were fitted with an extra pair of lifeboats forward at upper vehicle deck level.

Another 'before and after' comparison, this time of Viking Venturer *seen arriving at Cherbourg in the summer of 1985 as built and, two years later, leaving Portsmouth for Le Havre as rebuilt and with newly added P&O funnel design* (Author and Maritime Photographic).

Above   *The new bow sections for both pairs of Townsend Thoresen ferries re-built in Germany in 1985-86 were constructed in the form of a single hull and then separated in dry dock. Here the new bows for* Viking Valiant *and* Viking Venturer *are side launched into the River Geeste at Leche from the slipway where the 'Spirit' class vessels were also launched, but which was not able to accommodate* Pride of Dover *or* Pride of Calais *whose hulls were built in Bremen at the Vulkan Yard* (Townsend Thoresen).

Below   *Removal of the superstructure of the 'Super Vikings' was a more complicated task than with the 'Free Enterprise' vessels and was handled in two halves. Here, amid the Bremerhaven snow in January 1986,* Viking Venturer *parts company with the aft section of the superstructure, the main mast and funnels having already been removed* (Townsend Thoresen).

Bulky but businesslike! Viking Valiant *leaving Portsmouth for Le Havre in June 1986* (Miles Cowsill).

New twin-level ramps were provided in both Portsmouth and Le Havre for the enlarged ships although shore work had not been completed when *Viking Venturer* was ready to resume sailings after final attention to the passenger accommodation at Southampton. Until all was ready and the *Viking Valiant* returned early in July, the ship was used on the Cherbourg route. This did not prevent *Viking Venturer* from feeling the force of Townsend Thoresen's publicity machine when officially welcomed back to Portsmouth on 19 May, where the reception committee included an elephant!

With industrial troubles at both Felixstowe and Le Havre affecting Townsend Thoresen as 1986 opened, the company seized the opportunity to send *Viking Valiant* to Germany a little earlier than planned and the conversion operation, now down to a fine art by Schichau's work force, went without a hitch. *Viking Valiant* re-entered service on 3 July a week after *Viking Venturer* had finally switched to the Le Havre service. The £15 million investment in the two ships is expected to extend their working lives by at least ten years.

Viking Viscount and *Viking Voyager* were moved to Portsmouth to cover during the enlargement programme but are not likely to be rebuilt since their capacity is considered adequate for the Cherbourg route which attracts less freight traffic. Early in 1987 cabins were removed to allow the installation of Club Class lounges similar to those in their bigger sisters and as both types operate in and out of Portsmouth an interesting 'before and after' comparison is possible and in statistical terms the differences are detailed below:

	Viking Venturer *Viking Valiant*	*Viking Voyager* *Viking Viscount*
Built	Aalborg 1975	Aalborg 1976
Rebuilt	Bremerhaven 1985/6	–
Length	143.6 metres	128.72 metres
Width	19.81 metres	19.81 metres
Gross tonnage	14,760	6,387
Capacity	370 cars (900 lane metres)	275 cars (468 lane metres)
Passengers	1,316	1,200

Baltic Ferry/Nordic Ferry

Owner European Ferries/Monarch Steamship Co. **Flag** British. **Operator** P&O European Ferries. **Route** Felixstowe-Zeebrugge. **Built** Hyundai Shipbuilding, South Korea, in 1978/1979; rebuilt Wilton-Fiejenoord, Holland, 1986. **Gross tonnage** 18,732. **Net tonnage** 10,578. **Length** 151 m. **Width** 21.6 m. **Draught** 6.0 m. **Machinery** 2 Pielstick diesels of 11,475 hp. **Speed** 17 knots. **Passengers** 650. **Cabin berths** 184. **Vehicle capacity** 570 TEU. **Vehicle access** Bow and stern. **Former names**

Although registered in London, Nordic Ferry *was still on charter from Stena Line when pictured loading at Felixstowe for the freight route to Rotterdam Europoort in 1985* (Author).

Baltic Ferry: Stena Transporter (Stena Line 1978–9); Finnrose (Atlanticargo, charter 1980); Nordic Ferry: Merzario Hispania (Merzario Line, charter 1979).

Townsend Thoresen's passenger and vehicle service between Felixstowe and Zeebrugge, opened in 1974, was successful without ever fully exploiting the potential of regular ships *Viking Viscount* and *Viking Voyager* and it was not altogether surprising when, in 1985, the company announced plans to switch the two 'Super Vikings' to French routes from Portsmouth. A passenger element on the Belgian service, however, was maintained through the conversion of the freight vessels *Baltic Ferry* and *Nordic Ferry*. The latter ships were in use on the trailer service from Felixstowe to Rotterdam's Europoort which had been acquired, along with Transport Ferry Service, in 1971.

The service continued to operate under that name for a number of years and the vessels employed did not finally receive the orange Townsend hull colours until the winter of 1977–8. Three or four ferries continued in use until 1980 when the route was upgraded by a charter from Stena Line of two of the high capacity ro-ro ferries built in South Korea to the

Swedish company's acclaimed 'Searunner' design. The *Stena Transporter*, completed in 1978, became *Baltic Ferry* and a sister vessel delivered a year later direct to charterers Merzario Line as *Merzario Hispania*, was renamed *Nordic Ferry*. After alterations at Lloyd Werft to enclose the existing upper trailer deck and new superstructure containing cabin accommodation for 140 drivers, the ships were introduced in January and December 1980 respectively, each making a daily round trip and providing considerably greater freight space than the previous three-ship, six-trip service.

The invasion of the Falklands by Argentina in April 1982 resulted in *Nordic Ferry* and *Baltic Ferry* being requisitioned to sail to the South Atlantic carrying equipment and supplies for the entire army division transported by *Queen Elizabeth 2*. The *Nordic Ferry* was back in British waters during July and resumed work from Felixstowe late in August after a refit on the Tyne. Meanwhile, the *Baltic Ferry* remained at Port Stanley well into 1983 and could claim to have been the longest serving of the ferries called-up for the emergency since she did not finally arrive back in Felixstowe until April 1983, returning to service the following month.

Two lengthened 'Searunner' ships *Hellas* and *Syria* were chartered to stand in for the Townsend Thoresen twins and in 1986 the same two vessels were brought in again on long-term charter to take over the Europoort service.

The extent of the passenger accommodation provided on Nordic Ferry *and* Baltic Ferry *for their switch to the Felixstowe–Zeebrugge service is clearly seen in this view of* Baltic Ferry *leaving the Belgian port in June 1986, shortly after the funnel was repainted in the P&O colours* (Maritime Photographic).

They received the traditional TFS names of *Doric Ferry* and *Cerdic Ferry* when releasing *Nordic Ferry* and *Baltic Ferry* to go to Rotterdam to receive extensive passenger accommodation changes. New facilities were constructed at two levels on top of the previous container deck under a £10 million contract placed with the Wilton-Fijenoord yard at Schiedam.

The two ships which had been bought from Stena Line for £21 million in December 1984, each received tailor-made accommodation for 650 passengers arranged on two levels and featuring discrete lighting, deep pile carpets and decorations including selections of limited edition prints. A shopping boulevard leads passengers to a self-service garden restaurant and there is also a more intimate waiter-service brasserie with other main rooms including a lounge bar and a video lounge.

A total of 92 two-berth cabins are available, all with tea and coffee-making equipment and some with inter-connecting doors for family groups. This area is fully self-contained, the previous drivers' accommodation in the main superstructure block at the stern is retained and

the bridge also remains in its original position and was not moved forward. For the comfort of passengers each ship was also fitted with fin stabilizers.

Baltic Ferry went to Rotterdam in February 1986 and was joined by *Nordic Ferry* in the middle of March — by which time the Felixstowe services had been brought to a standstill by a dispute over the manning of the pair's successors on the Europoort route. *Baltic Ferry* moved to the Zeebrugge run on 23 May and the 'new look' operation with each ship making a daily round trip was completed when *Nordic Ferry* arrived from Rotterdam early in June and went into service the same night.

Pride of Dover/Pride of Calais

Owner European Ferries. **Flag** British. **Operator** P&O European Ferries. **Route** Dover-Calais. **Built** Schichau Unterweser, Bremerhaven, in 1987. **Gross tonnage** 26,000. **Net tonnage** Not available. **Length** 168.2 m. **Width** 27.8 m. **Draught** 5.85 m. **Machinery** 3 Sulzer diesels of 31,500 hp. **Speed** 22 knots. **Passengers** 2,300. **Cabin berths** 92 (freight drivers). **Vehicle capacity** 650 cars. **Vehicle access** Bow and stern.

The largest ferries ever built for a short sea service represent an investment of £85 million by European Ferries for the Townsend Thoresen operation and apart from technical refinement and points of consumer appeal to compete with both existing ferry opposition and any future English Channel fixed link, the *Pride of Dover*

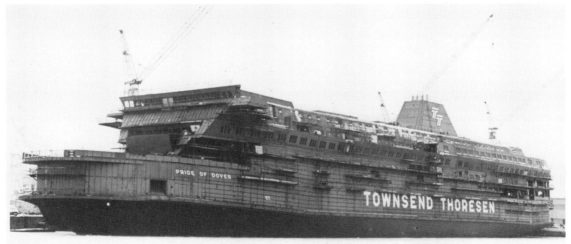

and *Pride of Calais* are claimed to have achieved greater cost effectiveness per freight unit transported than any previous vessels.

With the tunnel eventually likely to provide a new dimension of competition, Townsend Thoresen deliberately set out to enhance the travel experience of seaborne passengers with a philosophy much along the lines of the big Baltic combines and in some respects the interior ambience of the huge new ships is quite reminiscent of Viking Line's vessels with large scale use of mahogany and brass. The aim is to create an impression of giving travellers more than they pay for. The accommodation for 2,300 passengers is spread over two main decks with room below for a total of 650 cars on two complete decks, each with additional space on hoistable platforms.

Many modern ferries are launched or floated out of construction docks in a high state of completion but Townsend Thoresen's English Channel super-ferries almost reverted to more traditional practices. The hull of Pride of Dover *is seen entering the water on 20 September 1986. The superstructure was then added after the vessel had been moved to Schichau's main yard in Bremerhaven* (Townsend Thoresen).

Dover-Calais traffic took a tremendous leap forward from 1980 with the introduction of the *Spirit of Free Enterprise*, *Herald of Free Enterprise* and *Pride of Free Enterprise*, vessels of almost 8,000 tons which became known as the 'Spirit' class, and which had sufficient speed to make as many as five return crossings in a 24-hour period, taking up to 1,300 passengers and 350 cars a trip. They were built by Schichau

Unterweser, the Bremerhaven concern also responsible for another four Townsend new buildings in addition to the enlargement of the quartet already described, and it was logical that the German yard would be entrusted with the task of constructing the latest ships.

Obviously a lot of features from the 'Spirit' class were incorporated in the new vessels, but while they all took shape at Leche before a side launching into the Geeste, a tributary of the River Weser, there was insufficient space for the new 'Pride' twins to be handled in this way. The actual hulls were built in Bremen by the Vulkan Yard, one of Schichau's partners in a Weser shipbuilding and repair co-operative also including Seebeckwerft and Lloyd Werft.

Pride of Dover was launched by Mrs Hazel Parker, wife of the then executive director of European Ferries, on 20 September before being towed the few miles down the Weser to Bremerhaven for fitting out. This latter task was well on the way to completion when *Pride of Calais* arrived from Bremen following its own launching on 11 April, a ceremony performed by Mesdame H. Ravisse, wife of the chairman of the Calais Chamber of Commerce. *Pride of Dover* commenced sea trials during May 1987 and after preliminary visits to try out the newly-installed twin-level, double-width berths at both Dover and Calais, the ship officially entered service on 2 June, taking the key 10.30 departure from Dover. Sadly its debut was overshadowed by the loss of *Herald of Free Enterprise* two months earlier.

Apart from a choice of bars and lounge areas there is a wide range of eating options in-cluding a 55-seat restaurant with full silver service, two self-service cafeterias seating 292 and 204 respectively, plus a further 55-seat lounge/diner. A completely fresh innovation is a 180-capacity functions suite available for hire for anything from a sales conference to a wedding reception or private party. Duty free sales remain as a major attraction with passengers, especially day trippers, and the two ships each boast an extensive shopping complex including a supermarket, gift shop, news kiosk and exchange bureau. Freight drivers are not neglected and 46 two-berth cabins are available for their use. Interior design, in which there is much use of subtle colour combinations, soft lighting and multi-textured wall coverings, is the work of a German consultancy, with much of the furniture of Belgian manufacture while a Finnish company is responsible for some of the ceiling finishes.

The main propulsion machinery also reflects an international effort with the three low-consumption Swiss-designed Sulzer ZA40S engines built under licence by CCM in France. They produce 31,500 hp at 510 rpm for a service speed of 22 knots to maintain a schedule of 75-minute crossings. The rather unusual triple-screw arrangement first seen in the 'Free Enterprise' ships and used again for the 'Super Vik-

Townsend Thoresen emerged from the gloom surrounding the loss of Herald of Free Enterprise *at the beginning of June 1987 when* Pride of Dover, *pictured during trials, became the largest ferry ever operated on a short sea route between Britain and France* (Townsend Thoresen).

Pride of Dover, *pictured at its home port following a maiden round trip to Calais on 2 June 1987* (Author).

ings' and 'Spirit' class has been adopted once more.

Pride of Dover carried 250,000 passengers in its first six weeks of service and was joined by *Pride of Calais,* delivered in the full P&O blue hulled livery on 1 December.

Sealink British Ferries

Although the Bermuda-based American company Sea Containers Ltd received 37 ships and ten ports when paying £66 million for Sealink UK, the shipping and harbours operation of the British Railways Board in July 1984, the only true super-ferry included in the somewhat controversial transaction was the *St. Nicholas*. This vessel had been introduced on charter from Stena Line of Sweden a year earlier to bring a major improvement to the service from Harwich to the Hook of Holland, run jointly with the Zeeland Steamship Company (SMZ). Existing operators including European Ferries and P&O were ruled out of the bidding for Sealink at an early stage and after the withdrawal of other contenders including Trafalgar House and Ellerman Line, the only serious rival to Sea Containers was a consor-

tium including existing Sealink management and the National Freight Corporation.

Harwich Parkeston Quay, one of the ports acquired by Sea Containers as part of the takeover, is easily the most important passenger terminal on the east coast of Britain, with regular sailings to Holland, Germany, Denmark and Sweden maintained by the largest concentration of major ferry tonnage outside the Baltic. Parkeston Quay was established by the Great Eastern Railway and named in honour of its then chairman, Charles Parkes, in 1883, after authorities in Harwich itself refused to allow expansion of earlier facilities.

The railway interest centred on links with Holland, and in particular to the Hook of Holland. The traditional pattern of day and night services resumed after the Second World War, and it was not until 1968 that British Rail and SMZ each introduced a new vessel and inaugurated a full car ferry service using new berths provided at Parkeston Quay in a major reconstruction during 1967. The British *St. George* and its Dutch near-sister *Koningin Juliana* were joined in 1976 and 1978 by larger new units *St. Edmund* and *Prinses Beatrix*, traffic demand increasing to such an extent that for night sailings the ships often had to double up with the two British vessels sailing from Harwich and the SMZ ships running ex-Hook.

The route's resources were severely stretched from April 1982 when the 8,987 ton *St. Edmund*, then the largest Sealink ship, went to the South Atlantic with the Falklands Task Force. The vessel was subsequently purchased by the Ministry of Defence and retained on an Ascension-Falklands supply link under the management of Blue Star Line. Sold to Cenargo in 1985, she returned to ferry work in the Mediterranean during the summer of 1986. In the absence of *St. Edmund*, the *St. George* soldiered on as lone British representative until June 1983 when the Swedish-built *St. Nicholas* was introduced with some ceremony.

Three years later after SMZ introduced their impressive 31,000 ton *Koningin Beatrix* to supersede the *Prinses Beatrix* and a chartered relief ferry, Sealink chairman James Sherwood spoke of plans for the eventual replacement of *St. Nicholas* with one of a pair of new buildings of similar size and quality to the Dutch ship. However, no order materialized and before the end of 1986 it was confirmed that the original five-year *St. Nicholas* charter agreement with Stena Line had been extended with the addition of annual purchase options.

St. Nicholas

Owner Stena Line. **Flag** British. **Operator** Sealink British Ferries. **Route** Harwich-Hook of Holland. **Built** Gotaverken Arendal, Gothenburg, in 1982. **Gross tonnage** 17,043. **Net tonnage** 7,859. **Length** 149 m. **Width** 26 m. **Draught** 6.1 m. **Machinery** 4 Wartsila diesels of 15,360 hp. **Speed** 20.4 knots. **Passengers** 2,100. **Cabin berths** 1,061. **Vehicle capacity** 480 cars. **Vehicle access** Bow and stern. **Former name** *Prinsessan Birgitta* (Stena Line 1982–3). **Sister vessel** *Kronprinsessan Victoria* (Stena Line).

St. Nicholas started life as hull number 909 at the Arendal Yard in Gothenburg as the second of a pair of super ferries ordered by the Gothenburg-Frederikshavn Line (GFL) for its Sweden–Denmark service more usually advertised as Sessan Line. While the ships were under construction GFL had a brief tie-up with Tor Line before Stena Line, then a major competitor on the Gothenburg-Frederikshavn route, obtained a majority of interest in the spring of 1981. Stena also had large new ships on order from French builders but as these were well behind schedule the first of the Sessan sisters was completed and put on the route as *Kronprinsessan Victoria*, while work on No 909 was suspended. The following year it was decided to switch *Kronprinsessan Victoria* to the Gothenburg-Kiel overnight service and the ship was quite extensively altered with an upper car area converted into two decks of cabins. To fill the gap on the Frederikshavn route the go-ahead was given for completion of '909'.

Original plans for the ship to be called *Drottning Silvia* did not meet with official approval yet a royal name, *Prinsessan Birgitta*, was bestowed by the Princess herself in a ceremony at Gothenburg on 7 June 1982. After spending the summer on the Frederikshavn run, *Prinsessan Birgitta* was sent back to Cityvarvet in Gothenburg to have the passenger accommodation increased from 616 berths to 1,100 prior to being chartered to Sealink for the Harwich service and re-

Prinsessan Birgitta, near Gothenburg, while spending the summer of 1982 on the Stena Line service to Frederikshavn (Steffen Weirauch collection).

Above *When* Prinsessan Birgitta *became* St. Nicholas *in June 1983 the only changes were removal of the Stena Line funnel emblem and the addition of the Sealink name to the hull* (Kees be Bijl).

Left St. Nicholas *moving astern from the East Portal berth at Parkeston Quay where, at over 17,000 tons, it was the largest ferry using the port until the arrival of the Dutch* Koningin Beatrix *(Author).*

registered in Britain. New side access doors were cut in the hull and the two outer sections of the stern ramp were sealed as only the central segment fitted the portal berths at Parkeston Quay.

The ship, proclaimed to be the 'big one' in Sealink's lengthy publicity build-up, entered service on 9 June 1983, replacing the DFDS ferry *Prins Oberon* which had been standing-in on charter for Dutch vessels and was then switched to replace an ailing *St. George*, running on a temporarily extended certificate and suffering increasing mechanical problems. Six days later, in a ceremony at Parkeston Quay, the name *St. Nicholas* was adopted with Mrs Elizabeth Henderson, wife of the Sealink deputy managing director, doing the honours before over 300 invited guests were taken on a special cruise along the Suffolk coast.

Sealink and SMZ are among a minority of companies retaining a long established two class system, although in *St. Nicholas* the principal public rooms are open to all passengers apart from a first class lounge aft on Deck 7 where the centrepiece is a terraced bar seating over 500. One level higher, on Deck 8, the main restaurant operates on a carvery/cold table system with a small *à la carte* section. The area occupied by a restaurant on *Kronprinsessan Victoria* is a coffee shop in the Sealink vessel.

For a ship planned to run a service with a passage time of no more than three hours, the provision of around 400 berths in en suite cabins at two levels forward, together with a further 54 four-berth economy units below the car decks, was something of a surprise but proved quite a bonus following Stena Line's takeover and their decision to convert first *Kronprinsessan Victoria* and then *Prinsessan Birgitta* for full-scale overnight operation. The layout of the areas of new cabins differs

between them and in *St. Nicholas* some space was devoted to lounges with rest chairs.

Introduction of larger ships had little effect on crossing times, and the schedule evolved when the first car ferries came along has been retained with 6 hours 45 minutes allowed for day runs and 8 hours overnight. Apart from vehicles and passengers, the Hook route has retained its historical classic element with rail connections from the Hook to European and Scandinavian destinations. Trains running late can cause headaches and the British end of the service also often suffered from these problems prior to the electrification of the Harwich-London line.

When entering service, *Prinsessan Birgitta* wore Stena funnel colours but kept the intended Sessan Line white hull with a broad navy band, stepped down at the stern. On arrival in Britain a year later there were no

St. Nicholas *in the English Channel en-route from overhaul in Dunkirk to officially launch Sealink's new corporate colours with a first visit to Dover on 27 March 1984* (Sealink).

Following privatization and the purchase of Sealink by Sea Containers in the summer of 1984, the only alteration to the colours adopted earlier in the year was the addition of 'British Ferries' to the hull logo. It was applied to St. Nicholas *during a 1985 refit as seen in this view outward bound from Harwich in June 1986 (Scott Dennison).*

changes apart from the addition of the Sealink brand name to the hull and removal of the Stena funnel logo. By then, with privatization in prospect, the British Rail emblem had disappeared from ferry funnels and early in 1984 the *St. Nicholas* was chosen to officially unveil a new corporate livery, visiting Dover on 27 March, fresh from overhaul and repainting in Dunkirk. The main features of a dark blue funnel with gold bands and new style logo in light blue on the hull were retained after Sea Containers gained control later in the year.

Stoomvaart Maatschappij Zeeland (SMZ)

Founded in 1875, Zeeland Steamship Company is the oldest Dutch ferry concern and received much early support, both moral and financial, from Prince Hendrik, brother of King William III, to start close ties with the House of Orange that have been reflected down the years by the number of vessels to carry royal names. The

SMZ began regular services between Flushing and Queenborough in Kent, before later switching to Folkestone. The British port moved again in 1927 to Parkeston Quay and SMZ continued running to Flushing while the London and North Eastern Railway had used the Hook of Holland since the terminal was first opened in 1893. When sailings were restored in 1945 after the Second World War, the facilities at Flushing were wrecked and SMZ also centralized services on the Hook. Closer co-operation developed in the ensuing years with SMZ's ships marketed under the Sealink banner from 1970 and first appearing with the name on their black hulls three years later.

Prior to the introduction of the car ferries *St. George* and *Koningin Juliana* in 1975, with each vessel capable of making a full return sailing every 24 hours, the British ships tended to concentrate on the night service. The day crossings were in Dutch hands and the number of vessels needed was rather extravagant. The 9,356 ton *Prinses Beatrix* became the largest ferry on the route when introduced in 1978 and continued in front line service until the spring of 1986, latterly under charter from Brittany Ferries for whom the ship was later used to open a link between Portsmouth and Ouistreham as *Duc de Normandie*. With *Prinses Beatrix* re-registered in France and a Bahamian registered chartered ferry *Zeeland* as its running mate, SMZ moved into 1986 without a Dutch-flag ship in commission for the first time in its history.

By then a 31,000 ton ferry claimed to be ten years ahead of its time was nearing completion and had been ordered as a result of a strategic plan drawn up by SMZ which also made provision for a new third ferry berth at the Hook of Holland and all-round improvements to the passenger and vehicle facilities.

Koningin Beatrix

Owner Zeeland Steamship Co (SMZ). **Flag** Dutch. **Operator** SMZ. **Route** Harwich-Hook of Holland. **Built** Van der Giessen-de Noord in 1986. **Gross tonnage** 31,189. **Net tonnage** 15,170. **Length** 161.7 m. **Width** 27.6 m. **Draught** 6.2 m. **Machinery** 4 MAN diesels of 25,600 hp. **Speed** 22.3 knots. **Passengers** 2,100. **Cabin berths** 1,296 + 108 couchettes. **Vehicle capacity** 485 cars. **Vehicle access** Bow and stern.

The Zeeland Steamship Company's confidence in the future of the Hook of Holland-Harwich ferry link could hardly have been demonstrated in a more tangible form than the £40 million investment in the bulky but imposing *Koningin Beatrix*, introduced in April 1986 and replacing a pair of smaller vessels. SMZ's order went to Van der Giessen-de Noord who produced a ship evolved from rather drastically revised plans obtained from Seebeckwerft and based upon the German yard's super-ferry design. This concept had been evident in *Norland* and *Norstar* of North Sea Ferries and continued through the Olau Line sisters *Olau Hollandia* and *Olau Britannia* before culminating in the TT Line new buildings *Peter Pan* and *Nils Holgersson*. *Koningin Beatrix* has an external similarity to the latter vessels, delivered in the same year and 1987, although the hull itself probably leans more to the North Sea Ferries ships and was developed from the original single-ended loading to through-loading with bow and stern openings.

Until launched by Queen Beatrix of the Netherlands on 9 November 1985, all construction work took place indoors at the Van der Giessen yard's impressive covered slipway at Krimpen an der Ijssel, near Rotterdam, although the big occasion was not without controversy. Representatives of the builders were highly critical of the Dutch government, whose withdrawal of subsidies

Koningin Beatrix **on trial in the North Sea shortly before entering service on the Hook of Holland–Harwich route in May 1986. The family resemblence to TT Line's** Peter Pan **and** Nils Holgersson **is quite strong** (SMZ).

had just forced the yard to hand back another super-ferry order from North Sea Ferries partners Nedlloyd.

This did not prevent Van der Giessen from completing the all-welded, twelve-deck *Koningin Beatrix* on schedule. As early as launch day there was an indication of the considerably altered livery adopted by SMZ, with the hull sporting an all-white scheme which continued through the superstructure save for dark blue boot topping, decorative stripes and the names of the terminal ports with Dutch spelling on one side and in English on the other. There was no hint of the Sealink brand name. The traditional buff SMZ funnel with a black top separated by narrow bands in the Dutch national colours was retained but as befitted its regal status, *Koningin Beatrix* entered service with large crowns on either side of the casing.

The *Koningin Beatrix* can accommodate up to 2,300 passengers and for overnight sailings there are 1,296 beds in 559 cabins, all in forward locations and ranging from 61 in a luxury category to couchettes at the lowest level beneath the car decks. There are separate key public rooms with a 300-seat first class bar and lounge on Deck 8 and a 350-seat second class facility two levels underneath on Deck 6, each area boasting a dance floor where live music and entertainment is provided on most crossings. In between, on Deck 7, there are well over 200 seats in spacious *à la carte* and self-service restaurants, the latter incorporating a unique food dispensing system of a slowly rotating carousel screened off from the pantry where fresh food is supplied.

There are two main vehicle decks as well as space for cars at the after end of two higher decks. In the TT Line ships these upper car decks run full length with cabins on the outside, but in *Koningin Beatrix* there is a complete division with cabins taking all the forward space and cars towards the stern. All told the SMZ ship can take 485 cars, or 55 trailers and 220 cars with a separate hold for up to 50 trade vehicles.

Koningin Beatrix proved difficult to handle in port and there were some protracted early berthings. The ship damaged the specially adapted West Portal ramp at Parkeston Quay during a visit for berthing trials and, on 21 April 1986, when returning from an official inaugural cruise, it took almost two hours to get the giant alongside in an exercise needing tug assistance. Gradually, as personnel became more familiar with their charge, delays were eliminated. *Koningin Beatrix* loads via the bows in Harwich were an extra level had to be added to the quayside walkways to provide access for foot passengers.

Koningin Beatrix *off Felixstowe in May 1986. Note the Dutch spelling of the terminal port on the hull compared to the English version on the starboard side as seen in the previous picture* (Scott Dennison).

At the Hook of Holland works included provision of what is claimed to be Europe's biggest ferry berth at the eastern end of the quay with a 42 metre ramp capable of compensating for a tidal range of 8.6 metres. Major improvements have also been made to the terminals, which are connected to the berth by an embarkation tunnel fitted with conveyor-type sidewalks.

Olau Line (UK) Ltd

One of the first ferry links between Britain and Holland was established by the Dutch from Flushing to Queenborough in 1875 and while the traffic was lost from the Isle of Sheppey port to Folkestone and later Harwich, the original route was almost duplicated 99 years later when Olau Line commenced a freight service from Sheerness to Vlissingen in November 1974. The small ferry used on this occasion did have limited cabin accommodation and early in 1975 it was decided to open them up and carry passengers. The demand quickly made it necessary for a second vessel to be brought in on a daily service of two return sailings.

The company, formed by Ole Lauritzen, son of the principal of the major Danish shipping group, set itself a 1975 target of 40,000 passengers but actually carried 220,000 and larger ships were brought in from November 1975 and April 1976. Figures for 1976 showed a 100 per cent increase and the rapid growth continued into 1977 with sailings using the *Olau Finn* of 8,554 tons (on charter from Finnlines of Helsinki and originally one of a three-ship series for Swedish Lloyd) and another Scandinavian exile *Olau Kent* which, as *Apollo*, was lead ship of six built in the 1970s for Viking Line consortium members by Meyer Werft at Papenburg in West Germany.

From the beginning of 1978 Trampschiffarht-Gessellschaft MBH of Hamburg obtained a 50 per cent interest in Olau Line and subsidiary company TT Line were appointed as managing agents. With freight and passenger demand still increasing, a search for a larger multi–purpose vessel started but with nothing readily available a relief freight-only ship was used from May 1979. In September of the same year Trampschiffart acquired the other half of the Olau Line equity and within a two-month period announced the order of a new 15,000 ton ferry from AG Weser at Bremerhaven.

Olau Hollandia/Olau Britannia

Owner Olau Line (UK) Ltd. **Flag** German. **Operator** Olau Line. **Route** Sheerness-Vlissingen. **Built** AG Weser, Bremerhaven, in 1981/1982. **Gross tonnage** 14,990. **Net tonnage** 9,500. **Length** 153.4 m. **Width** 24.2 m. **Draught** 5.8 m. **Machinery** 4 Pielstick diesels of 15,300 hp. **Speed** 21 knots. **Passengers** 1,600. **Cabin berths** 938. **Vehicle capacity** 530 cars. **Vehicle access** Bow and stern.

Olau Line's emergence as a major competitor to the long-established Harwich-Hook of Holland joint service of Sealink and Zeeland Steamship Company was confirmed with the completion of *Olau Hollandia* in April 1981 which not only set new records in terms of size and capacity, but also offered facilities in a range and of higher quality than any other ship previously used in UK-Holland traffic. Since being joined by sister *Olau Britannia* in May 1982, the two ships have achieved a remarkable record for reliability and punctuality, crossing in six hours by day and nine overnight.

Builders AG Weser, now known as Seebeckwerft, drew on experience gained in the construction of *Norland* and *Norstar* for North Sea Ferries, although the interior design was based more on TT Line's 1970s pair *Nils Holgersson* and *Peter Pan* then running in the Baltic between Trelleborg and Travemunde. Almost half the passenger space is devoted to cabins, all located forward with public rooms toward the stern, and with scope for up to 1,600 passengers on daylight crossings. There is overnight accommodation for 900 in cabins and a further 220 reclining seats in four different lounges

Olau Hollandia's keel was laid on 5 May 1980, launching took place before the end of November and the completed ship was handed over on 21 March 1981, just eleven months from the start of work. By then a sister was taking shape and although it was at first stated that this would go to the TT service to release either *Nils Holgersson* or its twin for use between Sheerness and Vlissingen, the Hamburg administration relented and Olau received the second ship to bring about a completely balanced operation for the first time since the earliest days of the route.

Olau Britannia, launched in December 1981, was christened at Sheerness on 7 May 1982 by Princess Margaret and normally covers the overnight sailing to Holland, returning by

Olau Line's earlier dark blue hulls were abandoned when Olau Hollandia *came into service in May 1980, although blue and red flashes on the funnel and hull retain an element of the previous colour schemes* (Olau Line).

day from Vlissingen. Public rooms have been maintained to a high standard and there is a distinct German flavour to the style of the decor with hundreds of maps, prints and photographs on the walls of the passenger areas. Olau seek to provide onboard amenities at no extra charge to passengers and each ship has an attractive indoor swimming pool, fitness area, sauna and solarium.

The propulsion plant consists of four SEMT-Pielstick medium speed diesel engines built by Blohm and Voss driving twin screws through Lohamann and Stolterfoht reduction gearboxes. The installation was designed to enable just two engines to be used on the slower night crossings, while the service speed for day runs is 21 knots.

Since the two ships came into service there have been large scale improvements to the terminals at Sheerness and Vlissingen, the latter having two ramps. The ships berth stern on at the Dutch end and foot passengers also leave by a rear door connecting with walkways via a subway to the terminal building. Apart from the main deck and hoistable platforms accomm-

odating 550 cars or 60 cars and 65 trailers, there is also an upper car area normally used for carriage of trade cars on the westbound sailings.

When *Olau Britannia* and *Olau Hollandia* are eventually replaced it seems likely that they will be retained by TT Line and used to start a new route in Northern Europe.

New buildings (2)

Owner Olau Line (UK) Ltd. **Flag** German. **Operator** Olau Line. **Route** Sheerness-Vlissingen. **Builder** Seebeckwerft, Bremerhaven, delivery due in May 1989 and May 1990. **Gross tonnage** 35,000. **Net tonnage** Not available. **Length** 165.0 m. **Width** 29.0 m. **Draught** Not available. **Machinery** Not available. **Speed** 21 knots. **Passengers** 1,800. **Cabin berths** 1,880. **Vehicle capacity** 500 cars. **Vehicle access** Bow and stern.

Although the Sheerness-Vlissingen route is serviced by two of the most modern ferries linking Britain with the near continent, Olau Line began talking as early as 1985 about replacing *Olau Hollandia* and *Olau Britannia* with larger vessels by the end of the decade, chiefly to cater for growing demands of freight space. An order was anticipated once the new *Peter Pan* and *Nils Holgersson* were completed for parent company TT Line, and while steps were first taken to replace a pair of trailer ferries used on Baltic routes, contracts for new Olau Line tonnage were placed with Seebeckwerft for delivery in 1989 and 1990.

Above Olau Hollandia *berthed at Vlissingen where the double stern doors are used, with discharge via the* bow door at Sheerness. Lifeboat testing is in progress during this evening lay-over at the Dutch port (Author).

Below *After turning, off the Sheerness terminal,* Olau Britannia *makes a cautious approach to the ramp in May 1986* (Scott Dennison).

The new ships, whose construction costs will include subsidies from both the German Federal government in Bonn and the Bremen state authority, represent yet further refinement of the AG Weser/Seebeckwerft design developed from *Norland* and *Norstar* in the mid-1970s and continuing through the present Olau twins to the *Peter Pan* and its sister.

Without the operating constraints imposed by the harbour at Trelleborg, Olau's ships for the 1990s are to be both longer and wider than their two TT predecessors and measure in excess of 35,000 tons. They will carry at least 1,800 passengers with cabin accommodation on three decks forward with public rooms aft including three restaurants, a main dancing lounge and further bar and lounge areas. There will also be conference suites capable of seating as many as 300 on each ship.

Olau's traffic has levelled off at around 670,000 passengers a year but freight demand increased by almost 4,000 units in 1986 and whilst the total vehicle space on the new ships will be only marginally greater, they will be able to accommodate up to 120 trailers which is a 100% increase on the present ships which have consistently needed trailer ferry support in recent years.

No hint about names for the newcomers has emerged but it will hardly be a surprise if the TT's Baltic policy of retaining traditional names for the route is adopted and Sheerness sees the arrival of a second *Olau Hollandia* and *Olau Britannia*.

Fred Olsen Lines/ Kristiansands Dampskibsselskab

The Olsen family's shipping connections stretch back into the last century and the days of sail. Their first tonnage, the barque *Bayard* dating from 1861, beginning a tradition of giving vessels names starting with the letter 'B'. *Bayard*, a name taken from one of the most famous knights of chivalry, was also applied to the first Olsen steamship and new standards were set on the company's ferry services across the North Sea between Norway and Great Britain during the 1930s with the introduction of sister ships *Black Watch* and *Black Prince*. Both were lost in the Second World War, but more vessels of strikingly modern lines were built for the links from Oslo and Kristiansand to North Shields in the early 1950s.

The following decade brought close co-operation between Olsen Lines and Bergen Line with a pair of outstanding vessels built in 1966 for joint ownership and designed for summer North Sea ferry work under the names *Jupiter* and *Venus* before switching in the winter to an Olsen cruise service from London to the Canary Islands for which the ships became *Black Watch* and *Black Prince* respectively. Olsen later had a third example of the class, *Blenheim*, built to their own account for a summer Kristiansand-Harwich route, and winter cruising from London while *Black Prince* was also used to start a new Rotterdam–Canaries circuit. Vehicle deck space was fully utilized to bring huge quantities of fresh vegetables and fruit from the Canaries with a highly efficient form of containerized handling being devised.

In 1968 Olsen took over Kristiansands Dampskibsselskab, another Norwegian company established in 1899 and running across the Skagerrak from Norway to Denmark with Kristiansand-Hirtshals as the principal route. Considerable energy was devoted to the expansion of Hirtshals traffic and other seasonal routes were added including, in 1984, a revival of the weekly Harwich service that had been discontinued for several years following sale of *Blenheim* for use on day cruises from the United States.

By then the North Sea co-operation with Bergen Line had ceased, and for two summers DFDS chartered *Jupiter* and *Venus* to provide the UK-Norway services until the new Norway Line was formed to take over in 1985 using the *Venus*. The pattern was repeated in 1986 before the autumn saw each partner take one ship, Bergen selling *Jupiter* to Norway Line while Olsen retained *Venus*, which was refitted in Finland before commencing full-time cruising as *Black Prince*.

The Kristiansand-Harwich connection has always been part of a more wide-ranging roster. Its revival was possible following the return of what was then the largest Olsen vessel, the near 12,000 ton *Bolero*, after a spell on charter to Britain coming during a break in runs from Kristiansand to Hirtshals on the 'Skagerrak Express'. The same philosophy was applied when the company bought the well-appointed Baltic Ferry *Viking Song* in 1985 to start a new route from Oslo to Hirtshals as *Braemar*, one of the four weekly return trips being extended across the North Sea to Harwich and back.

Braemar

Owner Fred Olsen Lines. **Flag** Norway. **Operator** Fred Olsen Lines. **Route** Oslo-Hirtshals-Harwich. **Built** Wartsila, Turku, Finland, in 1980. **Gross tonnage** 13,879. **Net tonnage** 7,236. **Length** 145.0 m. **Width** 25.2 m. **Draught** 5.5 m. **Machinery** 4 Pielstick diesels of 24,000 hp. **Speed** 21.5 knots. **Passengers** 2,000. **Cabin berths** 1,223. **Vehicle capacity** 500 cars. **Vehicle access** Bow and stern. **Former name** *Viking Song* (Rederi AB Sally 1980–5). **Sister vessel** *Sally Albatross* (Oy Sally Line AB).

Fred Olsen ships have long been noted for having a distinctive and rather special onboard atmosphere which always came through particularly strongly in the *Venus* or *Jupiter*. Many regular travellers waited with some apprehension after confirmation early in 1985 that the company had bought Rederi AB Sally's *Viking Song*, a vessel specifically built for Baltic operation between Stockholm and Helsinki and running in the colours of Viking Line, a concern always noted for impact rather than subtlety when it comes to interior design. Fortunately the regulars had no need to worry for when Olsen unveiled their acquisition as *Braemar* it was difficult to imagine the ship had ever been used elsewhere.

Viking Song, launched on 23 March 1980, the same day as identical twin *Viking Saga*, was handed over late in August of the same year and joined its sister, commissioned two months earlier, on the overnight service linking the capital cities of Sweden and Finland. These ships were the first to bring the accommodation forward/services aft design concept to the Baltic, each having a total capacity of 2,000 passengers and overnight cabins for over 1,200 in two or four-berth units with private facilities including radios and a personal alarm call system.

Displaced by SF Line's *Mariella* in May 1985, the *Viking Song* went immediately to Fred Olsen and was refitted in Denmark before a June debut on the Kristiansand-Hirtshals route and the weekly Harwich service in place of *Bolero*, which had been sent on charter for a summer in the Baltic with Vaasanlaivat. The choice of *Braemar* revived the name of a British-built Olsen favourite which ran between Norway and the Tyne for over twenty years until 1975. The bronze figure–head and name signs from this earlier ship are prominently displayed on its 1980s successor, together with

Viking Line days with Viking Song *in the Stockholm archipelago during its time on the Helsinki service* (Anders Ahlerup).

the equally impressive bow bronze from the 1955 Olsen Mediterranean Lines vessel *Bergerac*.

The traditional Olsen passenger ship livery of grey hull, white superstructure and buff funnel was abandoned and *Braemar* seemed even larger than she had in red-hulled Viking Line days when she appeared all in white with a broad buff stripe at two levels along the passenger accommodation. Only the twin funnels, in time–honoured style, are buff with the Olsen house flag picked out in blue.

A number of improvements were made to *Braemar*'s passenger areas with the creation of a two-deck-high Tropical Garden easily the most impressive feature. The original night club on the eighth deck now forms the lower level of a huge area with grape vines and other exotic plants through which double stairs wind up to a glass-roofed upper gallery. By night the whole garden is transformed into a disco with stunning lighting and special effects — but somewhat more refined music is provided by a full orchestra on Deck 8 where there is also nightly cabaret-style entertainment.

Braemar's first Wednesday visit to Harwich was on 12 June 1985 and early in the summer Olsen announced that in September the ship would switch to a new year-round Oslo-Hirtshals shuttle with a weekend sailing leaving Oslo on Thursday evening extended into a round trip to Harwich arriving on Saturday mornings at Parkeston Quay. Return departure

to Hirtshals is late the same afternoon and after a Sunday evening call at Hirtshals, *Braemar* reaches Oslo early on Monday. This connection attracted growing support from Britain and is also popular with Norwegians as a five-days/four-nights mini-cruise. The Olsen company was also satisfied with its share of business out of Oslo from where Stena Line and Da-No Line already had long established Norway-Denmark services to Frederikshavn in addition to the Larvik Line route to Frederikshavn and Oslo-Copenhagen sailings by DFDS.

Some doubts were expressed as to *Braemar*'s suitability for winter use on the North Sea but the vessel has more than proved itself, with sensible scheduling allowing reasonable scope to compensate for any possible bad weather delays. The *Braemar* is powered by four Wartsila-Pielstick 12PC2 engines driving twin screws which enabled her to achieve 21.3 knots on trial. She is also equipped for bow and stern loading with space for around 500 cars or 60 trailers on two full-height vehicle decks with internal ramps.

Bolero

Owner Fred Olsen Lines. **Flag** Norway. **Operator** Fred Olsen Lines. **Route** Summer: Kristiansand-

What a difference a spot of paint makes! Viking Song *in the white and yellow colours of Fred Olsen Lines as* Braemar *and seen in Hirtshals Harbour in July 1986* (Anders Ahlerup).

Braemar leaving Hirtsbals for Oslo. The stern bronze is a typical Olsen embellishment and the glass roof of the ship's impressive Tropical Garden can be seen above the open deck with its well lined rails (Anders Ahlerup).

Hirtshals, Kristiansand-Harwich; Winter: Hirtshals-Stavanger-Bergen. **Built** Dubigeon-Normandie, Nantes, in 1973. **Gross tonnage** 11,344. **Net tonnage** 5,617. **Length** 142.1 m. **Width** 21.9 m. **Draught** 5.7 m. **Machinery** 2 Pielstick diesels of 15,000 hp. **Speed** 21.5 knots. **Passengers** 1,600. **Cabin berths** 620. **Vehicle capacity** 420 cars. **Vehicle access** Bow stern and starboard side. **Former name** *Scandinavica* (Stena Line, charter 1978–83). **Sister vessels** *Scandinavian Star* (Sea Escape, Florida); *Azur* (Paquet Line, chartered to Chandris 1987).

Although *Bolero* falls a little short of our 12,000 ton 'super–ferry' criteria, the vessel is worthy of inclusion as an example of a second-generation ferry that has displayed quite considerable versatility in a career embracing both cruising and more conventional ferry work, the latter including regular visits to British ports. The last of a trio of similar ships built at Nantes by Dubigeon Normandie, and laid down to the order of Fred Olsen Lines in 1971, she was launched as *Bolero* in June 1972 and completed in February of the following year.

By then the stern-loading near-sisters were *Eagle* on P&O's short-lived Southern Ferries service between England, Spain and North Africa, and *Massalia* on Paquet Line's Marseilles-Canary Islands route, but *Bolero* immediately went cruising, spending three years running for Commodore Cruise Lines from American East Coast ports to Bermuda and the Caribbean before switching in 1976 to the Nova Scotia link from Yarmouth to Portland, Maine.

While *Bolero* then returned to start European ferry work for the first time it is interesting that *Eagle* and *Massalia* eventually moved in the other direction to become cruise ships. Before the end of 1976 Olsen announced that *Bolero* would be placed on their year-round Kristiansand-North Shields service but business did not reach the expected levels and after replacement by a smaller unit in 1978, the vessel was chartered to Stena Line and renamed *Scandinavica* at the start of a three-year stint on the Gothenburg-Kiel service.

Bolero, as built, with swimming pool aft, in an aerial view while on charter to CN Marine in 1976 for the service from Yarmouth, Nova Scotia, to Portland, Maine (Fred Olsen Lines).

Bolero, already with bow and stern access, was next adapted for use on Olsen's Kristiansand-Hirtshals route with doors fitted on the starboard side forward of the superstructure and aft to give direct access to the upper car deck from special loading ramps at the two ports. In the winter the ship was used to develop a service from Hirtshals to Stavanger and Bergen. During the summer of 1984 the *Bolero* provided a midweek return sailing to Harwich. A spring and autumn cruise programme for the German market was announced in 1985, only to be cancelled through lack of bookings and following Olsen's purchase of *Braemar* the *Bolero* was chartered for a summer running across the Gulf of Bothnia for Vaasanlaivat.

By the time *Bolero* was back with Olsen the *Braemar* had been switched to the Oslo-Hirtshals-Harwich circuit and from 1986 the smaller vessel was again handling the winter run to Bergen which attracts massive trailer traffic, spending the summer months on the three-hour 'Skagerrak Express' between Kristiansand

and Hirtshals with a spot of midweek variety provided by the round trip to England, arriving in Harwich on Wednesday.

As built *Bolero* had a swimming pool aft, but this was decked over when the ship came back from North America. Cabin berths are available for almost 700 of a total passenger complement of 1,600 and these are supplemented by areas of rest chairs, a feature being the large number of outside cabins. The majority of A Deck is given over to a vast bar lounge area with a further Lido Bar aft, opening on to a sun deck. Located one level below is the main restaurant and separate cafeteria as well as the ship's shopping area.

Brittany Ferries

In 1972, the announcement of plans by a Breton vegetable farmers' pressure group to begin a ro-ro service to carry their produce from Roscoff to Plymouth was greeted with scarcely–disguised scepticism by shipping interests on both sides of the English Channel. Amazingly, they not only succeeded in starting the service on the first day of January 1973, but within a few months demands for passenger accommodation also resulted in the charter of another vessel. The company became known as

Above *The Bolero of the 1980s with the side ramps forward and aft fitted when the vessel returned from Stena Line charter work to go on the 'Skagerak Express'* (Author).

Below *An artist's impression of Brittany Ferries' first super-ferry, the 22,500 ton* Bretagne *due to be completed in the spring of 1989* (Brittany Ferries).

Brittany Ferries, and has been expanding in size and influence ever since.

Brittany Ferries' first purpose-built passenger and freight vessel *Penn ar Bed* was commissioned early in 1974 and two years later a larger Scandinavian ferry was purchased and used as *Armorique* to inaugurate a second route from Portsmouth to St Malo. A further new building, *Cornouailles*, joined the Roscoff-Plymouth route in 1977 and 1978 brought more expansion when *Armorique* inaugurated a twice-weekly Spanish link between Plymouth and Santander as well as a weekend connection between Roscoff and Cork. A Swedish ferry was chartered to replace *Armorique* at St Malo. It was purchased in 1980 and re-registered in France as *Prince of Brittany*.

The Portsmouth-St Malo route became a two-ship service each summer from 1980, when the much travelled Rederi Sally vessel *Viking 6* was chartered and introduced as *Goelo*. By the time the charter expired, Brittany had brought in a still larger Swedish flag ferry as *Quiberon* to take over the Spanish service from 1982, when *Armorique* slotted in to sail opposite *Prince of Brittany*.

The dramatic growth of Brittany Ferries was not straightforward. A £1 million operating loss in 1981 and predictions of even greater 1982 deficits prompted dramatic action, and a new holding company, including backing from the French government, Brittany local authorities, regional banks and industry, was formed and resulted in an injection of £8.5 million of new capital.

Back in the early days, new ro-ro facilities had to be provided for Britanny in both Roscoff and Plymouth, and before the end of the first decade more ambitious plans were announced for a fifth major service linking Portsmouth with a completely new ferry facility at Ouistreham near Caen. Having already bought *Quiberon* at the end of the initial charter, Brittany then bought Zeeland Steamship Company's Hook of Holland-Harwich vessel *Prinses Beatrix* which was refitted and renamed *Duc de Normandie* and used to inaugurate Ouistreham sailings in June 1986.

The demand for additional passenger and freight capacity on the Spanish route resulted in a lengthy search for larger tonnage and consideration of plans to 'stretch' *Quiberon* before an order was placed in June 1987 for the Brittany Ferries jumbo, the 22,500 ton *Bretagne*, to be delivered in 1989.

Bretagne

Owner Sabemen. **Flag** France. **Operator** Brittany Ferries. **Route** Plymouth-Santander, Plymouth-Roscoff, Roscoff-Cork. **Built** Chantiers de L'Atlantique, St Nazaire, France, for delivery in Spring 1989. **Gross tonnage** 22,500. **Net tonnage** Not available. **Length** 147.70 m. **Width** 26.60 m. **Draught** 6.0 m. **Machinery** Four x 12 cylinder Wartsila diesels, built in France. **Speed** 20.5 knots. **Passengers** 2,000. **Cabin berths** 1,088 + 500 Club Class seats. **Vehicle capacity** 600 cars (or 62 lorries and 200 cars). **Vehicle access** Bow and stern.

When Brittany Ferries first gave details of their projected Spanish connection the news was welcomed with an air of incredulity only little short of that prompted by company's creation a few years earlier. There seemed some grounds for the pessimism, however, the preceeding 18 months having seen the end of three established ferry services from Southern England to ports in Northern Spain. P&O's Southern Ferries route from Southampton to Santander ended in 1976 and during 1977 both Aznar Line (Southampton-Santander) and Swedish-Lloyd (Southampton-Bilbao) pulled out.

Brittany Ferries believed their service could succeed because of the shorter 24 hours sailing time from Plymouth (compared to more than 30 hours from Southampton), and also hoped that excellent motorways to the Devon port would play a part. They were proved correct on both counts and from 1979 the service was established on a year-round basis. Traffic potential quickly outstripped the 5,732 tons, 700 passenger *Armorique* and in April 1982 it was replaced by the 7,927 ton, 1,140 passenger *Quiberon*.

The summer schedule is particularly demanding and *Quiberon*'s week takes in two return sailings from Plymouth to Santander, a crossing to Roscoff to be positioned for the weekend Roscoff-Cork round trip, after which there is a sailing back to Plymouth before the cycle starts all over again, with no lay over in port exceeding any more than a couple of hours. Freight traffic to Spain has always been buoyant and it is not unusual for a trailer ferry to be used in the summer to relieve pressure on *Quiberon* when demands for car space is at its height.

Brittany sought tenders for a large multi-purpose ferry in 1986 and the order which finally went to Chantier de L'Atlantique at St

Nazaire in June 1987 was not without controversy, with claims that in its determination to secure the order for a domestic yard, the French Government was in breach of EEC rules concerning subsidies.

Although rather smaller than the current crop of new buildings for the Baltic, or the North Sea's recent newcomers, the *Bretagne* is designed to take 2,000 passengers with overnight accommodation for just over half the total, divided equally between two and four berth cabins, all with *en suite* facilities. In addition there will be 500 reclining seats in Club Class lounges.

Interior arrangements are in the hands of AIA de Nantes and the design team of Rondeau and Bidault who were responsible for the impressive alterations to *Duc de Normandie* following the vessel's purchase in 1986. *Bretagne* is to have a 250-seat à la carte restaurant, a 430 seat coffee shop, plus a 150-seat croissanterie, two main bars (420 seats) and a 150-seat wine bar. The ship will also have conference rooms, and as well as a large duty free supermarket there is to be an arcade of smaller boutiques.

Bow and stern loading doors will give access to two main vehicle decks with space for a total of 600 cars or a mix of 62 trailers and 200 cars. Main propulsive power is to come from four 12-cylinder Wartsila diesels, built under licence in France, with a projected service speed of 20.5 knots.

Ordered by Sabemen, one of the major controlling companies of Brittany Ferries, the ship is due to be delivered in the Spring of 1989 and will be operated on a long term charter basis.

Below *A striking view of* Quiberon, *the vessel at present employed by Brittany Ferries on its service from Britain to Northern Spain. Originally Swedish-owned and running between Malmo and Travemunde for Saga Line, it was first chartered by Brittany for the Plymouth-Santander run in 1982 and later purchased. When displaced by the new super-ferry* Bretagne *in 1989,* Quiberon *will switch to another Brittany Ferries route* (Brittany Ferries).

Chapter 3
The Danish invaders

Det Forenede Dampskibs Selskab, Akts (DFDS)

Founded in Copenhagen during December 1866, Det Forenede Dampskibs Selskab — the United Steamship Company — is now known universally as DFDS and its blue house-flag bearing a white Maltese Cross has been flown by more than 450 vessels, every one of which is represented in a remarkable picture gallery at the head office in the Danish capital. From the outset, international as well as domestic services were provided and, for many years until the mid-1930s, DFDS was involved in trans-atlantic traffic, carrying thousands of emigrants from Scandinavia to the United States.

Britain has long been Denmark's most important trading partner and regular services from the developing Danish West Coast port of Esbjerg, principally carrying cattle on the hoof, started as early as 1867 with just a handful of human passengers accommodated in spartan conditions almost as an afterthought. DFDS became one of the first users of Parkeston Quay, Harwich, when it was opened by the Great Eastern Railway in 1880 and have long been to the fore among innovative operators.

By the 1890s refrigerated cargo facilities brought an end to livestock transportation. From the mid-1920s DFDS were among the pioneers of diesel propulsion. This progressive trend continued as the demand for passenger and vehicle space developed until the company introduced the first drive-on North Sea ferry, the side–loading *England*, in 1964. By the time a near-sister vessel — the slightly larger *Winston Churchill* — was completed three years later it had bow and stern doors to take advantage of ramps by then installed at both Harwich and Esbjerg and in little more than a decade this pair had been superceded by even more capacious units still in the fleet today.

Traditionally, ships displaced from the Harwich-Esbjerg run have been introduced on secondary routes and while directly controlled domestic services within Denmark had disappeared, DFDS moved into the 1980s with year-

Above right *A super-ferry of the late 1960s,* Winston Churchill *photographed at Harwich after a maiden arrival from Denmark in June 1967, was typical of a series of ships introduced by DFDS in that period and although displaced from front line service it remains in the fleet for use on seasonal services from Esbjerg to North Shields and the Faroes and, in 1987, launched a series of spring and autumn cruises to the Norwegian Fjords and North Cape* (Alfred Smith).

Right *The largest vessel operated by DFDS was the 26,000 ton cruise-ferry* Scandinavia, *used for more than a year between Copenhagen and Oslo following the failure of Nassau-registered subsidiary Scandinavian World Cruises. Pictured at Copenhagen in March 1984,* Scandinavia *introduced the livery now applied to all the DFDS passenger ships but was sold in 1985 to Sundance Cruises, the American West Coast company in which the Silja Line partners EFFOA and Johnson Line have an interest. She was renamed* Stardancer *to run from Los Angeles to Mexico in winter and from Vancouver to Alaska during the summer months* (Author).

round connections Esbjerg-Harwich, Copenhagen-Oslo and, in the Mediterranean, Genoa-Tunis and Ancona-Alexandria — plus the seasonal links Esbjerg-Faroes and North Shields-Gothenburg.

Then came a period of uncontrolled expansion which almost proved disastrous, although it was not the acquisition of both Tor Line of Sweden and the West German Prins Ferries in 1981 — and incorporation in 1982 of former North Sea services provided jointly by Fred Olsen Lines and Bergen Line — that caused the problems. The damage was done by a costly bid to establish a cruise-ferry operation between New York and the Bahamas through a Nassau-based subsidiary Scandinavian World Cruises and using a luxurious purpose-built vessel, the 26,000 ton *Scandinavia*.

This service, with connections to Miami, never caught on and was abandoned within two years. For fourteen months *Scandinavia* was used between Copenhagen and Oslo before being sold at a loss to Sundance Cruises for work on the West Coast of the United States, serving Alaska in the summer and going south to Mexico for the rest of the year.

There were changes of key management personnel in the parent company as a result of the SWC fiasco and a major re-think on the ferry front saw both the Mediterranean services axed and the two vessels sold along with half a dozen other passenger and freight ships. Another casualty was the former Prins Ferries service from Harwich to Bremerhaven, dropped in 1984, and the next year DFDS pulled out of the UK-Norway trade in favour of the newly-formed Norway Line.

There was also better utilization of tonnage on the North Sea routes from Harwich and, overall, the drastic action proved effective with DFDS returning to profitability in 1986 as a new livery was introduced. DFDS also gained sufficient confidence to invest in larger tonnage for Harwich-Hamburg, the remaining ex-Prins Ferries service, from April 1987.

Dana Regina

Owner DFDS. **Flag** Danish. **Operator** DFDS. **Route** Copenhagen-Oslo. **Built** Aalborg Werft in 1974. **Gross tonnage** 12,912. **Net tonnage** 6,311. **Length** 153.7 m. **Width** 22.7 m. **Draught** 5.6 m. **Machinery** 4 B&W diesels of 17,600 hp. **Speed** 21.5 knots. **Passengers** 1,006. **Cabin berths** 1,006. **Vehicle capacity** 370. **Vehicle access** Bow, stern, side.

After commissioning half a dozen passenger vessels in the 8,000 tons range during the 1960s, all but one built in Italy, DFDS returned to Denmark for their first ship of the next decade which was not only substantially larger but strikingly different in appearance to its immediate predecessors which had all borne a strong family resemblance. Designed for year-round use between Esbjerg and Harwich, there was wide speculation that the newcomer from the Aalborg Yard would be called *Lady Clementine* but, fittingly, *Dana Regina* was the name bestowed by Denmark's Queen Margrethe II in a ceremony at Copenhagen on 1 July 1974, the vessel then making a flag-showing trip to Britain. *Dana Regina* became the largest ship to pass through Tower Bridge to visit London's Upper Pool and called for the first time at Harwich before crossing to Esbjerg and entering service with a maiden voyage on 8 July.

While earlier ships on the route had a measure of segregated accommodation, a legacy from construction at a time when two or three classes of passengers were carried, *Dana Regina* was a one class ship from the outset with berths for the full passenger complement of just over a thousand and most key public rooms on a single deck, an exception being the main bar/lounge which is at a higher level forward and was originally designed with a spiral staircase sweeping down to the restaurant immediately below.

Dana Regina served Harwich until October 1983 and had made more than 1,250 crossings when switched to share the Copenhagen-Oslo route with *Dana Gloria*, another vessel transferred from North Sea sailings as part of an economy drive. The arrangement hardly got into its stride before the huge *Scandinavia*, withdrawn from New York, appeared on the scene and charter work was found for *Dana Gloria*. Although at a disadvantage in terms of capacity and facilities running opposite a purpose-built cruise ship, *Dana Regina* was shrewdly marketed and attracted a following in her own right. In the spring of 1985, while awaiting the *Dana Gloria*'s return after the sale of the *Scandinavia*, the *Dana Regina* maintained the Oslo run single-handed.

Copenhagen-Oslo has always been a major revenue earner for DFDS and much of *Dana Regina*'s accommodation has been refurbished and updated since her introduction on the route. Regrettably, the spiral staircase was

Above   *Although many other large ferries of the era were ugly in the extreme, DFDS managed to combine traditional elegance and much increased capacity when introducing* Dana Regina *on the Harwich–Esbjerg run in 1974. Pictured on one of her first arrivals at Parkeston Quay,* Dana Regina *made more than 1,250 North Sea round trips before switching to the Copenhagen–Oslo service in 1983 (DFDS).*

Below   *In addition to bow and stern loading facilities,* Dana Regina *was also provided with side doors, which can be seen clearly in this shot of the vessel leaving Harwich (Author).*

removed to create more space in the lounge and restaurant and, during a 1986 refit a section of Boat Deck cabins was gutted to create a conference centre capable of seating over 100 or being divided into smaller units. During the summer peak, when conference business tails-off, the area is designed for easy conversion to couchette accommodation.

One legacy of the Scandinavian World Cruises operation was the application of its livery to *Dana Regina* and *Dana Gloria* during 1985 to foster a cruising image for the route and it was extended to the rest of the DFDS passenger vessels during 1986. As one of the features of the new colours is a predominantly white funnel, *Dana Regina* was provided with exhaust extensions to avoid too much discolouration of the funnel casing.

The change to a service within Scandinavia has not entirely ended *Dana Regina*'s North Sea appearances; the vessel is among several from the DFDS fleet to figure in annual autumn NATO exercises which have included several

Dana Regina*'s attractive lines lend themselves effectively to the DFDS cruising livery of the 1980s. Lying at Copenhagen in 1986, the vessel's exhaust extensions, provided to prevent discolouration of the funnel casing, are clearly visible* (Author).

visits to Harwich for troop movements and, in 1986, a first call at Southampton.

Dana Anglia

Owner Dansk Investeringsfond (DIFKO). **Flag** Danish. **Operator** DFDS. **Route** Esbjerg-Harwich. **Built** Aalborg Werft in 1978. **Gross tonnage** 14,339. **Net tonnage** 7,759. **Length** 152.9 m. **Width** 23.7 m. **Draught** 6.1 m. **Machinery** 2 Pielstick diesels of 15,445 hp. **Speed** 21 knots. **Passengers** 1,370. **Cabin berths** 1,249. **Vehicle capacity** 470 cars. **Vehicle access** Bow and stern.

Although DFDS usually built ships in pairs and returned to the Aalborg Yard for their next construction to join *Dana Regina* on the Esbjerg-Harwich run, it could not be described as a sister vessel in any way. Gone was the traditional row of lifeboats along the superstructure: life rafts stowed in containers alleviated the need for all but two pairs of boats carried well forward, and the tall, slender funnel positioned aft of the centre line created an impression of extreme length. Surprisingly, the new ship proved to be some three feet shorter than *Dana Regina* yet advances in interior design enabled over 200 additional berths to be provided together with a space for 200 more cars.

As with *Dana Regina* some four years earlier, the hull was launched without the bow section which was added later in dry dock and upon

Dana Anglia **making a dramatic evening arrival in the Pool of London on 3 May 1978, prior to being named next day by the Duchess of Gloucester. The DFDS flagship took the distinction of being the largest vessel to pass through Tower Bridge from** Dana Regina **which made a flag-showing visit to London four years earlier (DFDS).**

completion the new DFDS flagship sailed for London to be named *Dana Anglia* by the Danish-born Duchess of Gloucester. This ceremony took place whilst moored alongside HMS *Belfast* in the Pool of London on 4 May 1978, the vessel having taken the distinction of being the largest ship to negotiate Tower Bridge from *Dana Regina* in the process.

It was a tight squeeze, however. Even with extensions to the exhaust pipes removed there was a clearance of less than four feet. In fact *Dana Anglia* made a number of early service runs to Harwich before they were replaced. More recently, in February 1986, the exten-

sions were taken off again to allow the ferry to proceed up the River Weser while chartered in connection with NATO exercises. This was a rare break from routine crossings and not until January 1987 did *Dana Anglia* figure in commercial sailings on any route other than Esbjerg-Harwich when chartered for three weeks to provide overhaul cover, firstly for Sealink's *St. Nicholas* and then Zeeland Steamship Co's *Koningin Beatrix*, between Harwich and the Hook of Holland.

The public rooms layout introduced earlier on *Dana Regina* was developed in *Dana Anglia* and all facilities are connected by an attractive arcade on the port side — the only significant changes over the years being conversion of the original children's play area and adjoining meeting rooms into two cinemas.

After using Burmeister and Wain machinery for a succession of units, including *Dana Regina*, DFDS opted for Swedish-built SEMT-Pielstick engines for *Dana Anglia* and these

Left *The* Dana Anglia*'s tall funnel has become quite a landmark during alternate visits to Harwich for most of the year and with DFDS among the first companies to display their name on the sides of ships, this was how the* Dana Anglia *looked until 1986, the black funnel having a red band with the Maltese cross emblem on a blue disc (DFDS).*

Middle left Dana Anglia *was repainted in the new DFDS livery while in service during May and June 1986 but the result is rather less effective than on other ships, perhaps due to the funnel being positioned well aft of the centre line (DFDS).*

Bottom left *Berthed bow-on at her home port, Esbjerg, the modest size of* Dana Anglia*'s stern door, largely designed to fit the Harwich ramps, is evident (Author).*

have proved very reliable with the ship establishing a good timekeeping record on the twenty hour service. Normally *Dana Anglia* is turned round in a little over three hours at Parkeston Quay, Harwich, using the stern doors, with slightly longer allowed at the Danish end where discharge is via the bow ramp, these time spans being useful as considerable numbers of unaccompanied trailers are carried on this route.

As part of the financial re-structuring of

DFDS, the *Dana Anglia* was sold for 300 million DKr to Dansk Investeringsfond (Difko) in December 1982 and immediately leased back for ten years.

Dana Gloria

Owner DFDS. **Flag** Danish. **Operator** DFDS. **Route** Copenhagen-Oslo. **Built** Dubigeon-Normandie, Nantes, in 1974. **Gross tonnage** 12,348. **Net tonnage** 7,759. **Length** 152.4 m. **Width** 22 m. **Draught** 5.8 m. **Machinery** 4 Pielstick diesels of 17,650 hp. **Speed** 21 knots. **Passengers** 1,200. **Cabin berths** 769. **Vehicle capacity** 260 cars. **Vehicle access** Bow and stern. **Former names** *Wellamo* (EFFOA 1975–81); *Dana Gloria* (DFDS 1981–3); *Svea Corona* (Johnson Line charter 1983–5). **Sister vessels** *Orient Express* (British Ferries), *Pegasus* (Epirotiki Line). (All measurements before 1988 lengthening.)

Dana Gloria was one of a three-ship series ordered from the Dubigenon Normandie Yard at Nantes for delivery in 1975 to enable the companies operating as Silja Line to cope with rapidly increasing traffic across the Baltic bet-

The 'early days'. Dana Gloria *with the black and white funnel of Finland Steamship Company (EF-FOA) when employed on Silja Line's 'capital cities' route between Stockholm and Helsinki as* Wellamo *until early in 1981 (Anders Ahlerup).*

Above   *DFDS colours first time around,* Dana Gloria *immediately after joining the DFDS fleet and being placed on the Esbjerg–North Shields run year-round and with summer trips from North Shields to Gothenburg* (DFDS).

Below   *Dressed overall,* Dana Gloria *making a cautious first passage up the River Tyne at the start of a spell in which, at over 12,000 tons, she was the largest ferry regularly using North Shields* (DFDS).

Above *Falklands veteran* Norland *preparing to leave the North Sea Ferries berth in the Beneluxhavn at Rotterdam's Europoort on 20 April 1983 on the return leg of her first commercial sailing after almost a year in the South Atlantic* (Author).

Below Koningin Beatrix *lying in Harwich at the specially adapted Parkeston Quay East Portal Berth, following arrival on the day crossing from the Hook of Holland in August 1986* (Scott Dennison).

Above *North Sea Ferries achieved a dramatic increase in capacity on the Hull–Zeebrugge route by 'stret-ching' the* Norstar *and sister vessel* Norland, *seen soon after returning to service in June 1987. These 1975 stern loaders, displaced from the Rotterdam run by* Norsea *and* Norsun, *were refitted internally to standards similar to those of the new tonnage* (North Sea Ferries).

Below *Free Enterprise VI, one of the pair of Townsend Thoresen ferries from the Zeebrugge service rebuilt at Bremerhaven in 1985–86, going astern from its berth to turn in the Belgian port's inner harbour prior to a sailing to Dover during July 1987. The original passenger accommodation was lifted off in one piece and then replaced after the creation of a full upper vehicle deck. Early in 1988 the ship was renamed* Pride of Sandwich (Author).

Top right Dana Regina *approaching Parkeston Quay from Esbjerg in May 1983 towards the end of a nine-year association with the route* (Author).

Middle right *The newly repainted* Tor Britannia *alongside at Esbjerg in 1986. The forward side door, used to unload cars at Gothenburg, can be seen partially open to assist in vehicle deck ventilation* (Author).

Bottom right *Major 1987 acquisition for DFDS was the former Jahre Line vessel* Kronprins Harald *seen at St Pauli Pier on 3 April that year after being named* Hamburg *and prior to a debut on the service to Harwich next day* (Author).

Above *An impressive view of TT Line's* Peter Pan *on trials in May 1986 shortly before entering service on the Travemunde–Trelleborg run (Seebeckwerft).*

Below *Jahre Line's* Princesse Ragnhild *is one of the most elegant modern ferries and now runs opposite the new* Kronprins Harald *on the Oslo–Kiel service (Jahre Line).*

ween Sweden and Finland, and in particular on the Stockholm-Helsinki 'capital cities' route — although, by now, the others are also far from their early stamping grounds. Each of Silja's constituent companies took a vessel: *Dana Gloria* was launched for Finland Steamship Company (EFFOA) as *Wellamo* and was second into service. She began operations on the Stockholm-Helsinki route in July 1975, being preceeded by Bore Line's *Bore Star* — now *Orient Express* in Sealink colours — with Svea Line's *Svea Corona*, latterly cruising as *Pegasus*, completing the sequence.

Easily the largest ships of the period, even the capacity of *Wellamo* and her sisters could not keep pace with demand and by the dawn of the 1980s the first of the really colossal Baltic ferries was on order. Before the end of 1980 *Wellamo* was sold to DFDS with delivery to take place in May 1981 once the 25,000 ton *Silvia Regina* was commissioned. After overhaul and repainting in DFDS colours *Dana Gloria* visited Copenhagen for an official naming ceremony and then took over the Esbjerg-North Shields service which was stepped-up to year-round frequency, the vessel also making a twice-weekly trip to Gothenburg during the summer peak.

As accommodation and public rooms were already of the high standard demanded by Baltic passengers and included an indoor swimming pool and sauna unit, DFDS needed to make few changes to their acquisition which

Back again in the Baltic in 1984 and with the Silja seal's emblem once again in place on the hull, Dana Gloria *running between Stockholm and Turku under charter to Johnson Line of Sweden, having assumed the name of former sister ship* Svea Corona *(Anders Ahlerup).*

has berths for 769 of a total complement of 1,200. The levels of traffic to Esbjerg in the winter period proved disappointing and it was announced that from October 1983 *Dana Gloria* would move to the Copenhagen-Oslo service together with *Dana Regina* from the Esbjerg-Harwich run. The partnership was brief to say the least for, as previously recorded, the *Scandinavia* arrived on the scene and the *Dana Gloria* returned to Silja Line on charter, assuming the name of former sister *Svea Corona* and going on the Stockholm-Mariehamn-Turku run opposite the remaining member of the trio, *Bore Star* (by then *Silja Star*).

Once again the DFDS vessel found itself holding the fort until the arrival of much larger new tonnage, in this case the 33,000 ton *Svea*, and in two successive winters proved all over again its capabilities in the Baltic ice. Before resuming on the Oslo service from the beginning of June 1985, *Dana Gloria* was extensively overhauled and provided with conference facilities. Former lounge and disco areas on the sixth deck were also much altered to form a new grill restaurant, piano bar and separate disco, while the main bar aft was given a facelift

Left *When* Dana Gloria *resumed DFDS operations in 1985, partnering* Dana Regina *on the Copenhagen–Oslo link, she wore the then-new livery with diagonal stripes in three shades of blue on hull and funnel* (DFDS).

including new staging for the cabaret shows that have been one of the features of the route since the days of the *Scandinavia*.

DFDS have no direct rival between Copenhagen and Oslo yet there is considerable competition for Denmark-Norway traffic with three other companies serving Oslo from North Jutland ports. The DFDS sailings depart in each direction at 17.00 daily with arrival at 09.15 next morning: the vessels lie over until embarkation begins two hours before departure. In the last few years DFDS have made big efforts to market the Oslo service in Britain with through fares being offered at considerable discounts.

After considering several options to upgrade the Copenhagen-Oslo route DFDS announced in December 1987 that *Dana Gloria*'s capacity would be increased. The ship is being lengthened by the insertion of a new 22 metre mid-body section to give more cabins and boost restaurant, lounge and conference space. The work, out to tender as 'Super-ferries' went to press, will be completed before the summer peak of 1988. Then, in 1990, DFDS will take

delivery of the outstanding Baltic ferry *Finlandia* (fully described on pages 99–101) which has been purchased from Silja Line partners EF-FOA and will replace *Dana Regina*. It is expected that *Dana Gloria* will also eventually be displaced when *Finlandia*'s sister ship, *Silvia Regina*, becomes available in the early 1990s.

Tor Britannia - Tor Scandinavia

Owner DFDS/Dansk Investeringsfond. **Flag** Danish. **Operator** DFDS. **Route** Harwich-Esbjerg/Harwich-Gothenburg. **Built** Flender Werke, Lubeck, 1975/1976. **Gross tonnage** 15,656/15,673. **Net tonnage** 7,729/7,756. **Length** 182.3 m. **Width** 23.6 m. **Draught** 6.5 m. **Machinery** 4 Pielstick diesels of 45,600 hp. **Speed** 24.5 knots. **Passengers** 1,507. **Cabin berths** 1,416. **Vehicle capacity** 440 cars. **Vehicle access** Stern and side.

When DFDS finalized an agreement with Swedish Salen Group in the autumn of 1981 to purchase the North Sea activities of Tor Line it not only yielded passenger services from Sweden to Britain and Holland and an extensive ro-ro freight network, but also two of the most outstanding passenger ferries then in service,

Tor Britannia *and her sister were built with beam restricted to 23.6 metres to fit the lock linking their original Immingham terminal with the River Humber but it was still a tight squeeze as this 1975 shot proves* (Author's collection).

Tor Britannia and *Tor Scandinavia*, sister vessels which have made a major contribution to the revival of the Danish company's fortunes during the past five years.

Tor Line, originally a consortium of Swedish and Dutch companies including Trans-Oil of Gothenburg and Stockholm-based Rex Line (from whose initials the 'Tor' name was derived), began a triangular passenger and vehicle service linking Immingham, Amsterdam and Gothenburg in the mid-1960s using two specially constructed 7,300 ton ferries. Within a short time the Swedish founder companies were bought out by the Salen Group and Tor Line's tenth year was highlighted by the May 1975 debut of *Tor Britannia* which cost £13 million, and immediately set new standards on the North Sea in size, speed and comfort and could claim then to be the world's largest purpose-built car ferry.

The most valuable asset of *Tor Britannia* and identical sister *Tor Scandinavia*, also built by Lubecker Flender Werke and delivered in 1976, is their high speed. Designed to maintain 24.5 knots in North Sea winter conditions, they brought Sweden within 24 hours sailing of a

Tor Scandinavia *as she appeared when new, in 1976, at a time when Tor Line were using both Imm-ingham and Felixstowe for sailings to Gothenburg. In the summer of 1978* Tor Scandinavia *also main-tained North Shields–Gothenburg crossings, thus becoming the largest ferry to operate from the Tyne* (Author's collection).

British port for the first time and made the Gothenburg-Amsterdam trip in 22 hours with power in reserve from a line-up of four 12-cylinder Pielstick diesels producing 45,600 hp and a top speed of over 26 knots.

The UK-Holland connection had been dropped before the new ships arrived on the scene and although built to squeeze through the lock and into Immingham's non-tidal harbour they moved south when Felixstowe became the main passenger terminal leaving the South Humberside port to be developed for freight purposes. This also helped Tor Line see off the only serious competition on the passenger front, Swedish-Lloyd ending a long-established Tilbury-Gothenburg service in the autumn of 1977 after their slower and less well-equipped tonnage had been outclassed.

As completed, *Tor Britannia* had berths for 1,234 passengers but to meet demand a number of double cabins were fitted with two additional berths to raise total overnight capacity to 1,416 and these changes were incorporated in *Tor Scandinavia* while fitting out. Among the attractions for passengers were casinos and, a real innovation for ferries in the 1970s, cinemas. A partitioned area of the cafeteria was first used for showing major releases on *Tor Britannia* in 1975 and it marked the start for the company which now provides the screen entertainment on the majority of major ferries running from British ports.

While year-round services from Gothenburg

to both Felixstowe and Amsterdam were provided it was found that one ship could handle the traffic during the winter and in the early weeks of 1978 and the two following years *Tor Scandinavia* was chartered by the Dutch organization World Wide Expo and set off for lengthy tours including the Gulf States and Far East with the vehicle decks transformed into a massive floating exhibition hall for European manufacturers whose representatives were housed onboard and travelled with the ship.

In 1980 Tor Line entered into a brief liaison with the Gothenburg-Frederikshavn Line, trading as Sessan Line between Sweden and Denmark together with a Gothenburg-Travemunde link. *Tor Britannia* emerged from overhaul with the legend 'Sessan Tor Line' painted on the dark blue hull and Sessan Line's mermaid motif superimposed on the Tor Line funnel design of a symbolic wheel over waves. The move was mainly an attempt by Sessan to stave off a takeover by Swedish rivals Stena Line and at a later stage it seemed likely that both Sessan and Tor Line would be swallowed up by Sten A. Olsson's aggressive organization.

Eventually, DFDS bought Tor Line and Stena acquired Sessan, the most immediate change for *Tor Britannia* and *Tor Scandinavia* being a switch to Danish registry and adoption of the all white DFDS colour scheme which, if anything, emphasized their size. The two ships maintained the British and Dutch links in 1982, but in 1983 the British terminal was switched from Felixstowe to Harwich and the Amsterdam ser-

During the short-lived 1980 liaison, Tor Britannia *operated with the name Sessan Line added to the hull and the latter's mermaid logo was incorporated in the Tor Line 'wheel over the waves' motif* (Author's collection).

vice reduced to summer only.

At one stage when Scandinavian World Cruises was being set-up it seemed possible that *Tor Britannia* might be sent to the United States as *Scandinavia Star* to provide a Florida-Bahamas connection to cruises from New York by *Scandinavia*. In the end other tonnage was purchased and the two ex-Tor ships began to figure in Esbjerg sailings in the closing months of 1983 after *Dana Regina* was withdrawn to Copenhagen.

They really came into their own in the following year when the Gothenburg-Amsterdam sailings were dropped completely and an integrated schedule produced which, in the summer peak, enabled just three ships to handle daily departures from Harwich to Esbjerg and a sailing every second day to Gothenburg. This was possible because of the speed of *Tor Britannia* and her sister which alternate between Denmark and Sweden while *Dana Anglia* circulates continuously on the Esbjerg-Harwich link, the whole operation hinging on the ability of the Tor twins to make Esbjerg-Harwich return crossings in fifteen hours — four hours faster than *Dana Anglia*. This results in an 08.30 Parkeston Quay arrival and the vessel concerned is off to Gothenburg three

Above   Tor Britannia *looked even more imposing following acquisition by DFDS and adoption of their all-white livery in 1982* (Fotoflite).

Below   *DFDS were at pains to exploit the goodwill of Tor Line's name in Sweden and although both* Tor Britannia *and* Tor Scandinavia *were quickly switched to the Danish flag,* Tor Scandinavia *ran with the legend 'DFDS Tor Line' on either side of the hull until well into the summer of 1986 when the standard cruise-style livery was applied* (DFDS).

hours later, passing its sister ship, in-bound from Sweden, which then makes a quick turn round for the same evening's Esbjerg departure.

These intensive workings last from early June to the middle of August but there are also accelerated crossings from Esbjerg on Thursdays for much of the rest of the year when the two ships usually change rosters. During a 1985 low season sailing an attempt was made to make up time following weather delays, and *Tor Britannia* made the 342 nautical mile crossing between Esbjerg and Harwich in a record 13 hours 8 minutes, averaging 23.36 knots overall and gobbling up 22 gallons of fuel a minute!

While the ships have stood the test, the summer is a period of intense pressure for catering personnel especially with a range of different currencies handled each round trip and other anomalies caused by differences in Danish and Swedish law in areas such as onboard gambling. As no gambling is permitted on Esbjerg sailings the original casino on each ship was converted into a pair of cinemas: an arcade of gambling machines has been retained — but these remain locked on the Danish run.

One surprising feature for mid-1970s ferries was the lack of bow doors although this was more a reflection of ramp facilities then available than anything else and to compensate huge double stern doors were provided. There is also a side door forward near the starboard bow to speed discharge and loading of cars and smaller commercial vehicles at Gothenburg. The change of British ports to Harwich caused some problems with the Tor ships only able to drop one of their ramps when using Parkeston Quay's two older portal berths and if the ship is carrying anything close to full loads in either direction some nippy shore work is necessary to achieve on-time departure.

In Germany and Scandinavia DFDS were at pains to preserve the names of Prins Ferries and Tor Line for marketing purposes and the latter title was even revived for North Sea freight services. The Gothenburg passenger connection was sold heavily in Sweden as DFDS-Tor Line and this title was carried on the hull of *Tor Scandinavia* right up to application of the new livery in 1986. *Tor Britannia* was one of the first North Sea ships to appear in the cruising colours after an extended refit carried out in

There were further changes in 1986 when Tor Britannia *emerged from an extensive refit in the latest DFDS livery* (DFDS).

No DFDS ships look better in the new livery than the 'Tor' twins and although Tor Scandinavia *was last of the front line fleet to receive its stripes late in the summer of 1986, it was well worth the wait* (DFDS).

Copenhagen Frihavn which lasted well into January 1986. The refit included a lot of internal refurbishment with most cabins re-carpeted, the duty free shop extended and the disco, almost unchanged since new, upgraded and adapted to provide additional daytime lounge seating.

Tor Scandinavia, sold by DFDS to the Danish investment bank Difko in 1982 and chartered back for fifteen years, received the disco modifications while in service and the new colours were also applied progressively from mid-August during lay-overs in port as the schedules eased. There was some anxiety in the late spring when a crankshaft fault developed in one of the main engines and *Tor Britannia* handled most of the Gothenburg sailings with *Tor Scandinavia* covering the less demanding Esbjerg runs. The trouble was rectified sufficiently for the ships to interchange and share the accelerated crossings from Denmark but there was a week out of service in the autumn

before *Tor Scandinavia* finally stood down from the beginning of December to start a major overhaul and crankshaft replacement lasting until the middle of January 1987.

Hamburg

Owner DFDS Seacruises (Bahamas) Ltd, Nassau. **Flag** Bahamas. **Operator** DFDS. **Route** Harwich-Hamburg. **Built** Werft Nobiskrug, Rendsburg, West Germany, in 1967. **Gross tonnage** 13,141. **Net tonnage** 6,493. **Length** 156.4 m. **Width** 23.5 m. **Draught** 5.4 m. **Machinery** 2 SWD diesels of 17,650 hp. **Speed** 22.8 knots. **Passengers** 1,113. **Cabin berths** 1,029. **Vehicle capacity** 400 cars. **Vehicle access** Bow and stern. **Former name** *Kronprins Harald* (Jahre Line 1976-87).

After purchasing Prins Ferries in 1981, DFDS quickly became aware of the limitations of the German vessels providing sailings on alternate days from Harwich to Bremerhaven and Hamburg. The Bremerhaven route was dropped altogether from December 1982 and various schemes were considered to boost both passenger and vehicle capacity to Hamburg. Before the existing 5,830 ton chartered unit *Prinz Hamlet* was bought in October 1984, Irish Continental Line's 7,984 ton, 1,100 passenger *Saint Patrick II* was tried on charter but proved too slow and DFDS did not take up

Above   *After almost ten years with the grey hull and yellow funnel of Jahre Line as* Kronprins Harald — *as seen here at the Oslo terminal prior to sailing to Kiel—the handsome overnight ferry moved to the North Sea to start a fresh career for DFDS* (Author).

Below   *An aerial view of* Hamburg *which made a maiden departure from Germany to Harwich on 4 April 1987* (DFDS).

a purchase option. They also decided against 'stretching' the *Prinz Hamlet*, although tenders were sought from a number of European and Scandinavian yards for an operation that would have seen the hull cut vertically for the insertion of a new section amidships.

Another plan to obtain a large high–class vessel for the Copenhagen-Oslo route, which would have enabled *Dana Regina* to be released for Hamburg, also fell through. Finally, in the autumn of 1986, DFDS confirmed the purchase of a successful Norwegian vessel to commence Harwich-Hamburg sailings the following April. Their choice was *Kronprins Harald*, the handsome single-funnel ferry built in Germany for Jahre Line and used exclusively on its year-round Oslo-Kiel service since being delivered in 1967.

Long before the end of 1986 it was announced that *Kronprins Harald*, available because of Jahre Line's investment in a 24,000 ton new building from Finland, would be named *Hamburg* and DFDS had a little over a month to transform what had previously been a two–class ship to their specifications. The work was entrusted to Blohm and Voss in Hamburg and saw considerable alterations to the Restaurant Deck with 21 new four-berth cabins fitted in the area of the former forward lounge and additional berths added to a number of ex-

isting two and three-berth cabins, the exercise providing 110 extra berths in all and increasing overnight capacity to more than 1,000.

As built, *Kronprins Harald* berthed 850 passengers in first and tourist classes, but the vessel went back to builders Werft Nobiskrug at Rendsburg in 1982. A three-month overhaul included construction of 21 deluxe cabins at an upper bridge deck level. DFDS have designated these as 'Commodore Class' in line with the elite category including room service, complimentary mini bars and superior furnishings and fittings introduced with great success on other vessels from early 1984.

The *Hamburg*, now flying the Bahamian flag, left Hamburg for a maiden crossing to Harwich on 4 April 1987 and alternate day departures were provided until early November when the route's normal winter pattern of three round trips a week started. Although said to be capable of 22 knots, *Hamburg* has not matched the *Prinz Hamlet*'s fine record for year-round punctuality on the 21-hour crossings and late arrivals are not uncommon.

Hamburg *dressed overall and lying alongside St Pauli Pier, Hamburg, immediately after being named by leading German actress Heidi Kabel on 3 April 1987* (Author).

Chapter 4

Scandinavian connections

Fewer ships but with much increased passenger and vehicle capacity now dominate the ferry links from Germany's Baltic ports to Scandinavia and also those between Denmark and both Sweden and Norway. Apart from the limited pure passenger routes and long established train ferry connections, it was not until the post-war era that the vast expansion of wheeled freight traffic and growing tourism brought the large scale introduction of car ferries on both shorter crossings and overnight services. The potential of the ferry market attracted companies already active in other areas of shipping as well as concerns specifically formed to start fresh services and, in the last decade, as size and ferry capacities have grown dramatically there has been some consolidation with well-known names including Sessan Line and Saga Line disappearing.

Travemunde-Trelleborg Line (TT-Line), Hamburg

Formed in 1962, the Hamburg-based company's two-ship Travemunde-Trelleborg route developed sufficiently for a pair of new ferries, among the largest in northern Europe, to be introduced in 1974 and 1975. There was also an ambitious plan to expand into the English Channel market through a Southampton-St Malo service, using one of the earlier vessels from the Swedish run. This 1975 venture met with strong resistance in both Britain and France and although TT-Line showed off the chosen unit, *Mary Poppins* (originally *Nils Holgersson*) to the travel trade during a three-day visit to London and it did make an appearance at Southampton, the actual service never got underway.

Competition for traffic to Sweden increased from 1976 when Lion Ferry took over an existing Malmo-Travemunde link. Following the acquisition of Trave Line, another Swedish company running between Helsingborg-Copenhagen and Travemunde, Lion became Saga Line and posed an even greater threat. In 1980 TT and Saga merged and after a period of maintaining the previous individual services to both Malmo and Trelleborg, there was a concentration on Trelleborg and the former Saga passenger ships were sold.

Previously, in 1978, through its parent company Trampschiffahrt Gessellschaft MHB of Hamburg, TT–Line had also acquired 50 per cent of the Olau Line operation connecting Vlissingen in Holland with the British port of Sheerness and the remainder of the Olau Line equity was purchased from its Danish founder, Ole Lauritzen, in September 1979.

A pair of nearly 15,000 ton ships were ordered the following year: one for Olau Line, and her sister provisionally earmarked for TT-Line service. In the event, both went to Olau and the German sector had to wait until 1986 and 1987 when the very substantially larger *Peter Pan* and *Nils Holgersson*, continuing with names used consistently since the opening of the route, were delivered to TT-Line and partners Swedcarrier. The latter company was a subsidiary of Swedish State Railways, whose interest in ferry services to Travemunde goes back to the creation of Saga Line and before.

Like the Olau ships, the new TT-Line tonnage came from Seebeckwerft in Bremerhaven and shows quite a strong family resemblance to the earlier vessels, perhaps representing the ultimate development of a design first created in the mid-1970s with *Norland* and *Norstar* for North Sea Ferries.

Travemunde-Trelleborg Line were among the first operators to display their name on the hulls of ferries but for the present ships, perhaps to the relief of many potential passengers, the original 'TT-Linie' spelling is simplified to 'TT-Line'.

Peter Pan/Nils Holgersson

Owner TT Line/Wallenius Lines. **Flag** West Germany/Sweden. **Operator** TT-Line/Swedcarrier. **Route** Travemunde/Trelleborg. **Built** Seebeckwerft, Bremerhaven, in 1986/87. **Gross tonnage** 31,360. **Net tonnage** 16,200. **Length** 161 m. **Width** 27.6 m. **Draught** 6.2 m. **Machinery** 4 MAK diesels of 26,655 hp. **Speed** 21 knots. **Passengers** 1,700. **Cabin berths** 1,320. **Vehicle capacity** 550 cars. **Vehicle access** Bow and stern.

The most significant advance represented by *Peter Pan* and *Nils Holgersson* over their immediate predecessors of the same names and built around ten years earlier, is in vehicle capacity but while passenger totals are much the same, the accommodation overall is of far higher standard with berths available for virtually all, rather than under half, of a 1,600 com-

plement. In contrast to the older units which tended to be very crowded on busy crossings, TT's ships of the late 1980s seem able to absorb passengers and could, if pushed, cope with several hundred more.

Arrangement of the vehicle decks, capable of taking 550 cars or 120 trailers, is impressive and effective when turn-rounds of as little as 45 minutes are necessary in the summer peak when three journeys on the seven-hour crossing are scheduled in each 24 hour period. The ferries load via twin stern doors in Travemunde and discharge over the bows at the Swedish end with internal access to the various levels being gained by way of particularly wide ramps. In the winter months the sisters can be operated as one compartment ships taking maximum loads of freight and still around 800 passengers.

The 1,324 berths are spread through 490 cabins, most situated forward, with the recreation and service areas towards the stern on three decks. All passenger cabins are fitted with electronically coded locks and instead of cabin keys passengers receive special cards produced onboard and for which the actual codes are changed every voyage. The issue of food and drinks in the bars and restaurants is also performed with coded keys and the system ex-

Peter Pan became the largest passenger vessel registered in Hamburg when commissioned in May 1986 and visited the port before entering service between Travemunde and Trelleborg (Seebeckwerft).

When Nils Holgersson *entered service in March 1987 it was easily recognizable from sister* Peter Pan *by virtue of having brown lifeboats* (Seebeckwerft).

tends to the self-service cafeteria where customers use a plastic card to make selections and then receive a printed and fully itemized bill at the pay desk.

A total of four restaurants offer nearly 1,000 seats and, reflecting the tastes of a largely German clientele, there is greater demand for *à la carte* service than the Scandinavian buffet fare preferred on the big Baltic vessels. Internal styling is also unashamedly Teutonic in character with a lot of dark panelling and veneers that might even be considered a trifle dull by Viking Line standards.

Peter Pan was delivered by Seebeckwerft on 30 May 1986 having taken seventeen months from contract to completion and as the largest passenger vessel registered in Hamburg it paid a visit to the port before entering service. It had been assumed that the lead ship would be called *Nils Holgersson* following early disposal of the 1975 vessel of the same name. However, the existing *Peter Pan* became *Robin Hood* to release the name at the beginning of 1986 and ran in this guise for its last fifteen months before sale.

The new Swedish-registered *Nils Holgersson* was completed in March 1987 and first ran opposite *Robin Hood* while *Peter Pan* stood down for an overhaul before the two giant ferries began operating together. *Nils Holgersson* was sold on delivery by Swedcarrier to Wallenius Lines and then bare-boat chartered back for twenty years.

Hull design was the result of extensive tank tests at the Shipbuilding Research Institute in Vienna and one feature incorporated was an extremely bulbous bow. Models were also used to test manoeuvering qualities with the confined spaces in the port of Trelleborg especially in mind. In practice, the ships can be turned round within their own length using bow thrusters, full rudder and counter-rotating propellers.

Main propulsion is by four non-reversible four-stroke MAK engines, one pair acting clockwise and the other anti-clockwise through reduction gears. Total output is 26,655 hp at 500 rpm and a trial speed of 21.5 knots was achieved.

Jahre Line

Sea connections between Norway and Germany go back a long way with regular sailings between Oslo and Kiel recorded as early as 1847. But it was not until the years following the Second World War that trade really started to build-up, largely on the initiative of Norwegian shipowner Anders Jahre, then principally involved in the whaling industry, who started a ferry company bearing his name in 1961. A new 7,500 ton vessel called *Kronprins Harald* was ordered from Howaldtswerke in Kiel and by 1966 business had expanded sufficiently to justify an enlarged sister ship which was named *Princesse Ragnhild*, thus starting a tradition for naming the route's ships after the heir to the Norwegian throne and his sister.

For a number of years *Princesse Ragnhild* was used for cruising in the winter months until increasing tourist traffic, especially at weekends, necessitated a two-ship service throughout the year. The pattern of earlier years was repeated with the first new *Kronprins Harald* built by Werft Nobiskrug in 1976 and offering four times more vehicle deck space than its predecessor. In 1981 Jahre returned to HDW for an even larger second *Princesse Ragnhild*.

Jahre's reputation for high onboard standards was enhanced by these ships and they remain the only major Scandinavian operator with a two-class system still in operation. While most companies have service areas open to all passengers and charge different rates dependant on cabin facilities and position, Jahre Line also have separate lounges for first and tourist class travellers and a fare structure that reflects the exclusivity of the route. Prices for the nineteen-hour run are much higher than those of Stena Line for the Gothenburg-Kiel run or the DFDS Oslo-Copenhagen link — both taking about fifteen hours.

By the mid-1980s Jahre Line were looking to expand again and broke their association with the German builders when ordering the third *Kronprins Harald* from Wartsila's Turku Yard in Finland, for delivery late in March 1987.

Princesse Ragnhild

Owner Jahre Line, Oslo. **Flag** Norway. **Operator** Jahre Line. **Route** Oslo-Kiel. **Built** Howaldtswerke Deutch Werft, Kiel, in 1981. **Gross tonnage** 16,332. **Net tonnage** 10,375. **Length** 170.5 m. **Width** 24 m. **Draught** 5.8 m. **Machinery** 2 SWD diesels of 17,652 hp. **Speed** 22.2 knots. **Passengers** 896. **Cabin berths** 322 first class, 420 tourist and 154 couchettes. **Vehicle capacity** 600 cars. **Vehicle access** Bow and stern.

Apart from high onboard standards, Jahre Line has always been noted for turning out distinctively handsome ships and the second *Princesse Ragnhild*, handed over by HDW on 31 January 1981, maintained this reputation despite incorporation of modern design features including positioning of machinery — and consequently the funnel — well aft of the centreline. Like previous tonnage *Princess Ragnhild* appeared with a grey hull, white superstructure and a buff mast and funnel, the latter carrying the white Jahre houseflag with a blue cross and central white star.

The Jahre practice of placing first class cabins above the restaurant deck, and tourist accommodation below, was continued and berths are available for the entire passenger complement of 896, 320 in the first class category including

Jahre Line's reputation for using elegant ferries has been more than maintained since the introduction of the 16,332 ton Princesse Ragnhild *in 1981 (Jahre Line).*

A first glimpse of Jahre Line's radically altered funnel design, introduced for the new Kronprins Harald, *was seen in Oslo from January 1987 when running mate* Princesse Ragnhild *returned from refit by builders, HDW, in Kiel* (Gerhard Fiebiger).

Length 164.5 m. **Width** 28.4 m. **Draught** 6.5 m. **Machinery** 4 Sulzer diesels of 27,000 hp. **Speed** 21.5 knots. **Passengers** 1,432. **Cabin berths** 1,432. **Vehicle capacity** 700 cars. **Vehicle access** Bow and stern.

sixteen luxury cabins on the Bridge Deck, and 420 tourist berths and 154 couchettes. Most of the tourist accommodation is located on a complete Cabin Deck and only a small number of cabins are positioned below the vehicle space on the Upper Tween Deck towards the stern.

There is room for 600 cars or 43 18-metre trailers on the main and hoistable car decks. An unusual feature is the provision of two areas for carriage of more than 150 export cars on the Upper and Lower Tween Decks and reached by hoistable ramps from the Main Car Deck, the five-hour turn-round from 08.00 arrival at Kiel or Oslo to departure at 13.00 giving plenty of time for loading and discharge.

Princesse Ragnhild is powered by two Stork Werkspoor diesels and achieved 22.6 knots on trials. The vessel has bunker capacity to provide a range of 6,000 nautical miles at a service speed of 21 knots, the engines driving two-bladed skew back propellers via Lohmann and Stolterfoht reduction gears.

Kronprins Harald

Owner Jahre Line. **Flag** Norway. **Operator** Jahre Line. **Route** Oslo-Kiel. **Built** Wartsila, Turku, in 1987. **Gross tonnage** 31,122. **Net tonnage** 16,200.

Jahre Line's 25th anniversary year was marked by the order for its most impressive vessel to date and the largest to serve Oslo since the period when DFDS were running *Scandinavia* on the Copenhagen route. To coincide with the introduction of the latest *Kronprins Harald* the company's Oslo terminal and administrative headquarters at Hjortneskaia was completely demolished during 1986 and replaced with a substantial new building offering greatly improved facilities for passengers.

A new era also began afloat with *Kronprins Harald*'s maiden sailing from the Norwegian capital on 25 March 1987. The vessel's 1,432 berths, all cabins with private facilities, brought a substantial increase in capacity over its immediate predecessor and running-mate *Princesse Ragnhild*, and representing three times the number accommodated by the first *Kronprins Harald* which inaugurated the service in 1961.

Jahre's first Wartsila ship includes a number of features in layout and internal styling which are similar to the yard's Viking Line sisters *Mariella* and *Olympia*, most notably a stylish and wide connecting arcade on the starboard side of the restaurant deck. However, the two-class system will still operate and in the best

Top *Jahre Line's largest ferry to date,* Kronprins Harald, *with her striking new funnel design, on trials in the Baltic shortly before being handed over by builders Wartsila of Finland* (Wartsila, Turku).

Above Kronprins Harald *at Kiel shortly after entering service at the end of March 1987. The vessel enjoyed an excellent first year achieving high levels of cabin occupancy* (Gerhard Fiebiger).

ocean liner traditions the first class public rooms are forward and for tourist passengers towards the stern. This is also reflected in the positioning of the cabins with the main block of first class accommodation at the forward end of the superstructure on four different levels, two above the the service areas and two below, but with no cabins below car decks.

Both the first class lounge and the tourist aft saloon have live bands where travellers can dance away the evening hours and in addition to *á la carte* and Norwegian cold table restaurants there is also an English-style pub and a smart cafe from where parents can keep an eye on children in an adjoining play area. A conference centre seats up to 162 or can be divided into three smaller units, but Jahre have not thought it ncessary to provide the fitness centre, saunas and swimming pools now considered essential for Baltic ferries.

In line with current practice there is a mix of engines with *Kronprins Harald* powered by two Wartsila-built Sulzer V-12s and a pair of six-cylinder in-line units connected to reduction gearing in the so-called 'father and son' arrangement and capable of use in different combinations as operating conditions require. The service speed is 21.5 knots and, thanks to special engine design considerations within the hull form, the vessel consumes only the same amount of fuel on an Oslo-Kiel-Oslo circuit as the previous *Kronprins Harald* which is less than half its size.

The original artist's drawings showed the new ship with similar colours to the existing Jahre fleet and while the *Kronprins Harald* was launched with the traditional buff funnel, when delivered it introduced a completely new-look with a white funnel carrying the houseflag's blue cross and central star and with a blue stripe between the grey hull and white superstructure.

Unlike many companies who strive to maintain overnight services with equally matched vessels, Jahre Line has always coped quite adequately with ferries of different size and capacity and while fare levels are the same there has been a definite publicity effort to see that *Princesse Ragnhild* does not lose out to its new running mate.

Stena Line AB

No company has earned a greater reputation for expertise and versatility in every respect of ferry operations than Sweden's Stena Line, yet it was only as recently as December 1962 that a first passenger link was started with chartered tonnage between Gothenburg and Skagen in Denmark. Now, in addition to a fleet of nearly twenty vessels on passenger and freight services, Stena is also heavily involved in liner traffic, the offshore market, property development

The 1,118 ton, 800 passenger Poseidon, *completed in 1964, was one of the first purpose-built Stena Line ferries and over twenty years and several changes of ownership later still carried the initial of her original operator at the bow when pictured at Vlissingen (Anny de Bijl).*

and scientific research. The company has also moved into travel-related areas including the hotel industry.

The company took its name from founder Sten A. Olsson who began in 1939 with a small chartered cargo vessel named *Dan*, after his son. Today Sten Olsson is chairman of the Stena group's parent company Rederi AB Concordia and Dan Olsson is managing director, the ferry side of the organization having grown out of all recognition since the pioneering days of the early 1960s.

At an early stage Frederikshavn became the Danish terminal for the service from Gothenburg which saw its first new Stena passenger vessel in 1964 with a first purpose-built car ferry introduced in 1965, a year when summer routes between Tilbury and Calais, and from Stockholm to Mariehamn, were also started (lasting until 1967 and 1972 respectively). A German connection through Kiel was opened in 1967. Progressively larger ferries were added with a new route between Frederikshavn and Oslo started in 1979 when two huge day vessels were ordered from France for the Gothenburg-Frederikshavn traffic together with four overnight ferries from Polish builders for the German service and possible additional routes.

Stena's main rivals for traffic to Denmark and Germany, the Gothenburg-Frederikshavn Line, first established in 1936, and best known as Sessan Line, also had two substantial new ferries on order but the possibility of serious overcapacity was avoided in 1981 when, following a short tie-up with Tor Line, the majority of GFL's shareholding was bought by Stena and a new company, Stena Sessan Line, was born. It was something of a blessing in disguise. Stena's own new tonnage on order from Dunkirk builders was late and the Sessan ships entered service for Stena. The *Kronprinsessan Victoria* began running between Gothenburg and Frederikshavn in 1981, before switching to Gothenburg-Kiel when sister vessel, *Prinsessan Brigitta*, appeared a year later. Stena's own giants were finally completed in 1983 but the frustrations were only beginning as far as the four Polish ships were concerned with delay following delay until, in the autumn of 1986, two orders were cancelled. The first ship, *Stena Germanica*, finally appeared in the spring of 1987 and was due to be joined by the *Stena Scandinavia* in 1988.

Quite apart from ferry services, Stena have

been highly successful in the charter business, building both freight and passenger tonnage specifically for this market including freight ro-ro's of the 'Searunner' and 'Searider' designs, as well as a quartet of 1975 passenger ships. All the latter were subsequently sold, two to Canadian National, one to Sealink British Ferries — now running as *St. Brendan* on the Irish Sea — and another to RTM of Belgium to be employed between Ostend and Dover as *Reine Astrid*. During the 1970s Stena also pioneered the practice of cutting passenger ferries horizontally to raise the superstructure and provide additional height on the vehicle decks.

In 1983, when a further new route from Frederikshavn to Moss in Norway opened, the Stena-Sessan name was dropped and the company became Stena Line AB. Stena Line also acquired two further existing ferry routes between Sweden and Denmark serving Grena from Helsingborg and Varberg. Since 1985 services on these routes have been trading as Lion Ferry and maintained by tonnage originally built for Sessan Line.

Kronprinsessan Victoria

Owner Stena Line. **Flag** Swedish. **Operator** Stena Line. **Route** Gothenburg-Kiel; Oslo-Frederikshavn from summer 1988. **Built** Gotaverken Arendal, Gothenburg, in 1981. **Gross tonnage** 17,062. **Net tonnage** 10,053. **Length** 149 m. **Width** 26 m. **Draught** 6.1 m. **Machinery** 4 Wartsila-Vasa diesels of 15,360 hp. **Speed** 20.4 knots. **Passengers** 2,100. **Cabin berths** 1,374. **Vehicle capacity** 500. **Vehicle access** Bow and stern. **Sister vessel** *St. Nicholas* (Sealink British Ferries).

After being well-served for almost a decade by the 1,400 passenger Danish-built sisters *Prinsessan Christina* (1969) and *Prinsessan Desiree* (1971), GFL ambitiously ordered two 2,100 passenger ferries from the Arendal Yard in Gothenburg. The first was launched on 15 October 1980 as *Kronprinsessan Victoria*, named in honour of the eldest daughter of King Carl Gustav and Queen Silvia of Sweden, who attended the ceremony. This took place during the short-lived connection between Sessan Line and Tor Line, but Sessan ceased to exist as an independent company in 1981, two months before the ship's completion.

The 'Sessan' title originated from the nickname of GFL's first building *Kronprinsessan Ingrid* of 1936, with Gothenburg taxi drivers reputedly among the first to use the

Above *After launching at Gothenburg,* Kronprinsessan Victoria, *wearing Sessan Line markings, being moved from the Gotaverken Arendal building dock prior to naming by Queen Silvia of Sweden in October 1980* (Author's collection).

Below *After the take-over of Sessan Line* Kronprinsessan Victoria *quickly adopted Stena Line colours and is seen in 1982 when running on the Gothenburg–Frederikshavn service* (Stena Line).

abbreviation. From then it became part of every GFL vessel's name and despite the amalgamation with Stena it was in white and dark blue Sessan colours that *Kronprinsessan Victoria* made its maiden sailing to Frederikshavn on 13 April 1981, technically chartered to Stena.

The newcomer's capacity for 700 cars or 70 lorries, and that of two Stena ships rebuilt in 1977, enabled the three-and-a-half hour Frederikshavn route to be covered by three ships instead of the five needed in the days of separate operations. Surprisingly for a comparatively short crossing, *Kronprinsessan Victoria* was also provided with 400 berths in cabins with en-suite facilities as well as over 200 couchettes. The public rooms were also on a grand scale with three restaurants, the largest seating 470, and a very impressive 600-seat terraced bar fronted by a stage and dance floor.

After some doubts Stena pushed on with the completion of *Kronprinsessan Victoria*'s sister (fully described earlier as *St. Nicholas*) and by the time it appeared as *Prinsessan Birgitta* in June 1983, *Kronprinsessan Victoria* was settl-

ing into a new role as an overnight ferry on the fifteen hour Gothenburg-Kiel run. In preparation for its debut *Kronprinsessan Victoria* had been sent to Arendal's City Yard in Gothenburg earlier that year for a nine–week conversion of the upper car deck into cabins which boosted the total number of berths to 1,374.

Kronprinsessan Victoria also emerged from the refit in Stena colours and is due to remain on the Kiel service until replaced by the second of the new Polish-built overnight ferries *Stena Scandinavica*, after which a transfer to the Frederikshavn-Oslo route is anticipated. In the early days of the Kiel service which involves

Both Stena Line and Sessan Line had separate terminals in Gothenburg but following amalgamation in 1981 Stena concentrated Danish sailings on their own facilities at Mastuggskajen, while the former Sessan base at Majnabbe was renovated to serve the Kiel service. Here Kronprinsessan Victoria *is alongside following the switch to the German route in 1983, as* Stena Danica *passes outward bound for Frederikshavn (Stena Line).*

departure in each direction at 19.00 and arrival next morning at 09.00, the vessel reaching Germany also made a daytime round trip to Korsor in Denmark, but these stopped when *Kronprinsessan Victoria* moved to the route as it was considered too large to use the Danish port. However, during Gothenburg lay-overs, there are occasions when Kiel ships are used in the summer months for special day sailings to Frederikshavn.

Kronprinsessan Victoria has a service speed of 20.4 knots from four Nohab Wartsila-Vasa V-12 engines and three smaller Warsila-Vasa auxiliary engines which are designed to use the same grade of heavy fuel, thus simplifying bunkering arrangements.

Stena Danica/Stena Jutlandica

Owner Stena Line. **Flag** Swedish. **Operator** Stena Line. **Route** Gothenburg-Frederikshavn. **Built** Normed, Dunkirk, in 1983. **Gross tonnage** 16,494. **Net tonnage** 7,744. **Length** 152.2 m. **Width** 28 m. **Draught** 6.3 m. **Machinery** 4 Sulzer diesels of 25,743 hp. **Speed** 20 knots. **Passengers** 2,300. **Cabin berths** 96. **Vehicle capacity** 600. **Vehicle access** Bow, stern and side.

By the 1970s ferries capable of carrying vehicles on more than one deck with connections by internal ramps and loading and

The side-loading facilities developed by Stena Line during the 1970s are clearly seen in this view of Stena Danica *after the superstructure was raised by 2.3 metres. Displaced by a larger new vessel of the same name,* Stena Danica *was chartered to RTM to operate between Ostend and Dover as* Stena Nautica *and from early in the summer of 1987 switched to the Dieppe Ferries service to Newhaven as* Versailles *(Bertil Soderberg).*

discharge through doors at the bow or stern were common, although height restrictions usually meant that only cars could be carried on the higher levels. In 1977, Stena set about fully utilizing this capacity and sister ships *Stena Jutlandica* and *Stena Danica* were subjected to a revolutionary rebuilding in which they were cut horizontally and the entire superstructure raised by some 2.3 metres to create a full upper deck. At the same time and just as significantly, side doors were provided to allow independent loading from the higher deck to fixed bridges on shore.

The system worked well and was included in the design of the first genuine super-ferries for the Gothenburg-Frederikshavn route ordered from Chantiers du Nord et de la Mediterranee (Normed) at Dunkirk in 1979, provisionally for delivery in 1981 and continuing with the names

Above *Stena Line's French-built twins for the Frederikshavn service,* Stena Jutlandica *and* Stena Danica, *with the latter on the Masthuggskajen terminal's main ramp (Stena Line).*

Below *Operating in ice conditions is certainly not confined to the Baltic but* Stena Jutlandica *is hardly in-convenienced by the elements when leaving Frederikshavn in February 1986 (Anders Ahlerup).*

of the rebuilt ships. Construction took longer than anticipated and lead ship *Stena Danica* was not ready for trials until January 1983 when mechanical problems arose and the scheduled delivery was put back until the end of February. A naming ceremony took place at Gothenburg on 27 February with first service runs next day. *Stena Jutlandica* was christened in Frederikshavn on 24 April 1983 and began commercial crossings the following morning.

Each ship carries 2,300 passengers and has 1,800 lane metres of vehicle space with eight lanes on each of the vehicle decks and the sight of lorries and trailers coming off the upper deck down spiral ramps at Gothenburg or Frederikshavn is especially impressive. Even with such vast numbers of passengers and vehicles to be handled, turn round in 45 minutes is accomplished on the majority of sailings and during the summer peak eight return crossings are provided in every 24-hour cycle and all but two round trips are covered by the *Stena Danica* or *Stena Jutlandica*.

To the unsuspecting passenger the impact of the onboard atmosphere of these ships can be quite overwhelming, catering almost

Contrasts in stern ramp design at Frederikshavn, with Larvik Line's Peter Wessel *and Stena's* Stena Danica *in adjoining berths. The Norwegian ferry's smaller outer doors connect directly to the upper vehicle deck but* Stena Danica *has separate side doors for the higher level* (Anders Ahlerup).

unashamedly for fugitives from Sweden's strict licensing laws intent on enjoying themselves. Two decks are given over to bars and restaurants together with a hall boasting batteries of gambling machines that looks like something from a Las Vegas hotel lobby. The duty free supermarket is huge with a row of no less than nine check-out positions, including one of extra width to take the wheelchairs of disabled passengers!

During 1986 the passenger areas were rebuilt in *Stena Jutlandica* to enable increasing numbers of day trippers to be handled and Stena Danica was due to receive similar upgrading early in 1988. This route is responsible for around three million passengers every year—or three-quarters of the entire Stena total.

Stena Germanica/Stena Scandinavica

Owner Stena Line. **Flag** Sweden. **Operator** Stena Line. **Route** Gothenburg-Kiel. **Built** Stocznia I.K. Paryskiey Gdynia/1987/Stocznia I.K., Gdansk 1988. **Gross tonnage** 30,244. **Net tonnage** 14,092. **Length** 175 m. **Width** 28.5 m. **Draught** 6.6 m. **Machinery** 4 Sulzer diesels of 33,098 hp. **Speed** 22 knots. **Passengers** 2,500. **Cabin berths** 2,272. **Vehicle capacity** 700 cars. **Vehicle access** Bow, stern and side.

Stena Line's Gothenburg-Kiel service has really been worked by a succession of stop-gap ships since the end of the 1970s despite orders for the quartet of overnight ferries from Poland. At the

Ordered in 1979, completed in 1987! Stena Germanica, first of Stena Line's much delayed ferries from Poland, finally arriving in Gothenburg in February 1987 (Stena Line).

time of that order a pair of 7,000 tonners built in Yugoslavia was in use, and when one of them, *Stena Scandinavica*, was sold in 1978 to Irish Continental Line to become the since-lengthened *Saint Killian II*, Stena chartered the Fred Olsen Lines ferry *Bolero* which ran as *Scandinavica* until 1981. In that year this vessel was replaced by *Prinsessan Birgitta*, acquired with Sessan Line and then running between Gothenburg and Travemunde. Stena closed that route and renamed *Prinsessan Birgitta* the *Stena Scandinavica* and it remained in use until the much-delayed first Polish vessel, *Stena Germanica*, was finally commissioned in April 1987.

The Stena strategy had been to upgrade the German sector with the first Polish pair and then consider either new routes or charter options for the remaining two. But things went sadly awry with materials shortages and at times a chronic lack of labour putting construction of two ships at Gdansk and the other two at nearby Gdynia, further and further behind schedule. Ownership of number one in the series, provisionally named *Stena Scandinavica*, was transferred in 1985 under a leas-

ing agreement to the British company Barclays Leasing and at the same time Stena pressurized the I.K. Pary yard into sub-contracting for the Swedish company Skanska to complete construction.

Late in the summer of 1986 Stena announced their intention of exchanging names between *Stena Scandinavica* and the number two ship, *Stena Germanica*. At the same time they cancelled the orders for ships three and four, to have been named *Stena Baltica* and *Stena Polonica* and which had hardly progressed beyond the bare hull stage of construction. Progress with *Stena Germanica* was then rapid and the ship made a long awaited first appearance in Gothenburg on 23 February 1987 with final fitting out and provisioning completed before a naming ceremony on 5 April and the maiden sailing to Kiel next day.

When ordered, the Polish ships were expected to be of around 20,000 tons but under the changes in measurement of gross tonnage that came into force during their construction this figure has now jumped to 30,244 tons. Despite the five-year delay before delivery *Stena Germanica*'s interior fittings are of the latest design, Stena taking advantage of the various hold-ups to monitor developments and incorporate new features. A total of up to 2,500 passengers can be carried — with overnight accommodation of 2,272. There is a huge increase in vehicle capacity over previous ships with 1,475 lane metres of space available to take up to 700 cars on two decks of full trailer height which each have additional platform decks. Twin stern and single bow ramps are provided and the main upper vehicle deck is served via shore ramps to doors forward and aft on the starboard side and a single forward port side entrance.

During a sailing in *Stena Germanica's* first season the interior of the vessel struck me as being cavernous and rather lacking in atmosphere, an impression probably fostered by the sheer scale of public rooms. Three main bar and lounge areas each accomodate over 350 passengers while the 'Vier Jahresiten' à la carte restaurant handles almost 500. With a large percentage of *Stena Germanica's* 619 cabins having four berths there were some capacity problems in the summer peak when one or two passengers often occupied cabins with four berths. As a result it is planned to use some of the upper deck vehicle space to provide a range of extra two berth cabins and *Stena Scandinavica* is likely to be converted in the same way.

When running at full speed, *Stena Germanica* experienced some vibration, especially towards the stern, and modifications or a complete change of propellers was expected in a first annual overhaul in the Spring of 1988.

As planned, *Stena Germanica* ran opposite *Kronprinsessan Victoria* during its first year and is due to be joined in April 1988 by *Stena Scandinavica*. The decision to switch names between the sisters was motivated by marketing considerations as it was felt that there would be less impact from introducing a new ship with the same name as the smaller unit it was replacing.

Larvik Line

Larvik Line came into being as Larvik-Frederikshavnfergen in October 1936 and introduced a small but nevertheless advanced vessel named *Peter Wessel* during the following year. Car capacity was no more than 60 or 70 yet there were both bow and stern doors, a factor which attracted the interest of Captain Stuart Townsend, founder of Townsend Brothers Ferries, when Larvik Line, struggling to make ends meet in 1939, were prepared to consider offers for their ship. As it was, the start of the Second World War prevented any purchase but not before Townsends had been left in no doubt that the bow door would have to

be welded shut before there could be any consideration of a certificate for English Channel service between Dover and Calais.

Peter Wessel was left to re-open the route following the war and also served Frederikstad at times before finally being replaced by a new building of the same name in 1968. A third *Peter Wessel* was commissioned in 1972 and Larvik Line also chartered to provide extra capacity during the 1970s. The company moved into the super-ferry league in 1984, when paying a reported 244 million Swedish crowns for Goltandsbolaget's *Wasa Star*, which, true to tradition, also became *Peter Wessel*.

The previous ship was first chartered to Zeeland Steamship Company (SMZ) for a stint on the Hook of Holland-Harwich run as *Zeeland* before being sold to Stena Line and placed on services from Frederikshavn to Moss and Gothenburg as *Stena Nordica* in May 1986.

Peter Wessel

Owner Larvik Line. **Flag** Norway. **Operator** Larvik Line. **Route** Larvik-Frederikshavn. **Built** Oresundbolaget, Landskrona, Sweden, in 1981. **Gross tonnage** 14,919. **Net tonnage** 8,380. **Length** 142.3 m. **Width** 24 m. **Draught** 5.5 m. **Machinery** 4 B&W diesels of 21,476 hp. **Speed** 21 knots. **Passengers** 2,000. **Cabin berths** 1,142. **Vehicle capacity** 515. **Vehicle access** Bow, stern, side. **Former names** *Wasa Star* (Vaasanlaivat, charter 1981–3); Karageorgis Lines, sub-charter 1984). **Sister vessel** *Visby* (Gotlandsbolaget).

In contrast to Frederikshavn where *Peter Wessel* is regularly in the company of Stena Line's big vessels, the Larvik Line flagship towers over the modest terminal in its home port and by day or night makes an impressive sight when coming up the fjord and swinging in a wide circle off the berth before reversing to the ramp. The fourth ship to carry the name of the famed Norwegian maritime hero is far and away the largest ever owned by Larvik Line and operates successfully despite a somewhat nomadic earlier existence.

The second of a pair of jumbos ordered by a reluctant Rederi AB Gotland under Swedish government pressure and originally to have been named *Gotland*, the ship was charterd to Vaasanlaivat while still under construction and was launched as *Wasa Star*, entering service across the Gulf of Bothnia between Sundsvall and Vaasa in June 1981. The Vaasa company, then owned by Enso Gutzeit, was less than enamoured with *Wasa Star*'s performance in

Above *Two views from the chequered early days of the ferry now enjoying a more settled career as* Peter Wessel. *The vessel is first seen in Vaasanlaivat colours as* Wasa Star *during 1983 and then a year later whilst running in the Eastern Mediterranean on charter to Karageorgis Lines, whose emblem appears on the funnel* (Martin Lochte-Holtgreven and Antonio Scrimali).

the winter ice and after continuing through the summer of 1982 the vessel was withdrawn and laid-up at Sundsvall. A sub-charter to Karageorgis Lines took *Wasa Star* to the Adriatic and a summer 1983 debut in Greece-Italy traffic between Patras and Ancona. During this period Karagerogis funnel colours were adopted but the name was not changed. Disagreements between Vaasanlaivat and Karageorgis arose in the autumn of 1983 and there was a sudden recall to Sweden where a further spell of inactivity began in Landskrona.

Before the end of the year Larvik Line had bought the ship and it left lay-up at Landskrona early in January 1984. *Wasa Star* finally came into service between Larvik and Frederikshavn on 3 March. On this route the ship takes up to 2,000 passeners on the six-hour crossing with over 1,000 berths, mainly in forward four-berth units. For night sailings the journey time is extended to between eight and nine hours. Like sister ship *Visby*, amenities include a stylish 204-seat cinema and sauna/fitness complex beneath two complete car decks together with considerable areas of seating in the main saloon and cafeteria. Yet I have found the *Peter Wessel* lacking in character — although the overall im-

Above right Peter Wessel *leaving Frederikshavn for Larvik in July 1986* (Anders Ahlerup).

Right *DSB giant* Peder Paars *lying over between sailings at Aarhus in July 1986* (Scott Dennison).

pression is perhaps clouded by the inevitably noisy Norwegian trippers who usually seem intent on consuming the maximum possible quantities of alcohol before dashing ashore to Frederikshavn's supermarkets!

Danske Statsbaner (DSB): Danish State Railways

It is hardly surprising that a kingdom of many islands such as Denmark boasts highly efficient internal and international ferry connections. While the greatest number of routes are maintained by Danish State Railways and form vital cogs in the national transport network, private enterprise companies also figure on both the domestic front and in services to Sweden and West Germany. Most of the DSB crossings are of a fairly short duration and whether taking road vehicles exclusively, or a mix of rail and road units, are covered by intensively worked but quite small ferries.

The DSB's first ships to exceed 10,000 tons were a trio of train ferries for the Great Belt service between Korsor and Nyborg which are still among the largest in their particular sphere and are compared later with major Swedish and German train ferry tonnage. Features of the high passenger standards achieved in these ships were incorporated in a pair of near 20,000 sisters commissioned by DSB for its longest crossing, the three-hour run between Kalundborg and Arhus which, while exclusively a passenger and road vehicle service, still provides important rail connections from North Jutland to Zeeland and Copenhagen.

Peder Paars/Niels Klim

Owner Danske Statsbaner (DSB). **Flag** Danish. **Operator** DSB. **Route** Kalundborg-Arhus. **Built** Nakskov 1985/1986. **Gross tonnage** 19,763. **Net tonnage** 6,180. **Length** 134 m. **Width** 24.4 m. **Draught** 5.5 m. **Machinery** 2 x MAN/B & W diesels of 16,490 hp. **Speed** 19.3 knots. **Passengers** 2,000. **Cabin berths** 148. **Vehicle capacity** 331 cars. **Vehicle access** Bow and stern.

The Kalundorg-Arhus crossing was always something of a poor relation to the shorter Great Belt run and remained virtually a classic passenger route until the introduction of the first of a pair of drive-on ferries in 1960. The same ships were still operating over 20 years and an estimated 22 million passengers later

Niels Klim making a careful stern approach to the berth at Kalundborg following a crossing from Arhus in August 1986 (Author).

and DSB was anxious to revive the route and attempt to win back traffic lost to the slickly run shorter operation of DFDS subsidiary Mols Line. Mols Line had appeared on the scene in 1983 and was a serious rival for long distance passenger business, with ferries taking express coaches running right through from Copenhagen to Arhus and vice-versa in a joint Mols/coach company venture.

Even so, some key figures in DSB's marine heirarchy would have been happier if the two ferries of almost 20,000 tons ordered from the Nakskov Skibsvaerft had received rails and gone instead to the 'Bee Line' route from Rodby to Puttgarden in Germany, but political influences won the day. Major shore works were necessary in both Kalundborg and Arhus and the new ships broke a long sequence of royal names for major DSB ferries when handed over in October 1985 and May 1986 as *Peder Paars* and *Niels Klim*, taking the names of characters from one of the best known works of the

Foot passengers wait by the ramp as vehicles go aboard Peder Paars *in a typically relaxed Arhus embarkation* (Scott Dennison).

Danish author Ludvig Holberg.

Some voices were raised in protest over the suitability for a ship of the name *Peder Paars*, who as a fictional merchant travelling to Arhus was beset with problems that prevented him from ever arriving! The criticism seemed prophetic as the new ferry had a number of hair-raising scrapes at Arhus and sustained damage in a series of collisions with the berth. *Niels Klim* also had its share of bumps in the early stages, main problems arising from wind resistance to 3,200 square metres of side surface area.

The DSB system of manning each ship with five crews whose eight-hour work period on a three-days-on, two-days-off cycle just covers a complete round trip, also meant it took a long time for the different bridge teams to familiarize themselves with the handling of their 134 metre charges. These imposing ferries can take 2,000 passengers and 331 cars, or thirty 18-metre trailers on the main deck and 152 cars on an upper deck connected by internal ramps.

Passenger accommodation is spread over two decks and thanks to main public rooms opening off central corridors the overall impression, especially in the three-deck central square, is most un-shiplike. The restaurants and seating halls are all quite compact and even the main cafeteria with over 300 seats is split into several sections.

A big effort to court business travellers is very evident with fully equipped writing rooms offering a range of facilities including typewriters, copiers, a computer terminal and pay telephones capable of receiving incoming calls. For executives wanting more privacy there are also individual office cabins with typewriters and telephones. There are also 72 two-berth cabins with private facilities under the car decks and DSB have made an effort to utilize them for round trip conference packages.

The new ferries and good train connections from Kalundborg have restored the route as a serious rival to the fast Inter-City services set-up via the Great Belt train ferry and, either way, journey times from Arhus to Copenhagen is around five hours.

Deutsche Bundesbahn (DB)

The train ferry service from Puttgarden to Rodby was jointly established by the German and Danish State Railways in 1963 to provide a new direct link between Western Europe and Scandinavia. A temporary service had operated between Grossenbrode and the existing Danish ferry port of Gedser for around twelve years while rail connections to Puttgarden and Rodby were improved and the terminal facilities established.

The 19 km crossing takes one hour and since it roughly follows the route taken by migrating birds it is advertised by the Danes as the 'Bee Line' and in Germany as the 'Vogelfluglinie', both the DSB and DB providing ships for the service with the German contribution significantly increased in 1986 when by far the largest ferry to date was commissioned.

Karl Carstens

Owner Deutsche Bundesbahn (DB). **Flag** West Germany. **Operator** Deutsche Bundesbahn. **Route** Puttgarden-Rodby. **Built** Howaldswerke, Deutsche Werft, Kiel, in 1986. **Gross tonnage** 12,820. **Net tonnage** 3,860. **Length** 164.8 m. **Width** 17.35 m. **Draught** 5.92 m. **Machinery** 6 MAK generators and 2 Siemens propulsion motors. **Speed** 19.6 knots. **Passengers** 1,500. **Cabin berths** None. **Vehicle capacity** 405 rail line metres plus 156 cars. **Vehicle access** Bow and stern.

The 'Bee Line' is a true multi-purpose route with ferries designed to handle railway traffic on the main deck with separate car space on an upper deck. Traditionally, the contribution from DB has been two vessels with the Danes providing a further four to cover over thirty return sailings a day. The largest Northern European passenger/train ferry came into being after the DB's administration in Hamburg acted to replace the veteran *Theodor Heuss*, dating from 1957, placing an order with HDW in Kiel for a ferry a full 20 metres longer than its immediate predecessor, the *Deutschland*, of 1972.

The keel of Yard No 211 was laid in HDW's Kiel-Gaarden Dock in July 1985 and the hull floated out in January 1986. The vessel was named *Karl Carstens* in honour of the former German president in a ceremony performed by his wife, Dr Veronica Carstens, in Kiel on 2 May. The actual service debut came from Puttgarden on 1 June when the *Theodor Heuss*, also named after an ex-Federal president, was retired from passenger service after 29 years — although the old-timer was subsequently brought back to run with rail and road freight only.

The new ferry has three-track stern loading to fit the ramp at Puttgarden and the rails are interlaced for discharge through a single track-width bow visor at Rodby. Up to fourteen standard passenger coaches can be accommodated, or a mix of rail and road vehicles including lorries and coaches. There is access to the separate car deck taking around 150 standard sized cars via shore ramps to three side ports.

The needs of 1,500 passengers are catered for on a full deck immediately above, with a restaurant, buffet, bar and additional amenities including an information desk, bank, boutique and duty free shop. For such intensively used ships the onboard standards of service and general cleanliness on the 'Bee Line' are very high and even in the middle of the night fresh hot food is always available.

Karl Carstens provides an interesting comparison with other major Scandinavian train ferries, notably the Swedish *Trelleborg* of 1982 which also has road/rail capacity and the three

Above *The 'Bee Line' route's largest ferry, the German flag* Karl Carstens, *introduced in May 1986* (Deutsche Bundesbahn).

Below *Swedish State Railways' 10,882 grt* Trelleborg *has served the route from Malmo to Sazznitz in the DDR since completion in 1982. In 1987 she helped to establish records in all areas of traffic covering rail passenger and freight, as well as cars and road freight vehicles* (Swedish State Railways).

latest Danish Great Belt ferries, *Dronning In-grid* (1980), *Prins Joachim* (1980), *Kronprins Frederik* (1981), all designed specifically for rail traffic and also loading via the bows only. The Swedish and Danish vessels all date before changes in the measurement of gross tonnage and, once again, the most accurate assessment is obtained from their respective dimensions and capacities:

	Karl Carstens (DB)	Trelle-borg (SJ)	Great Belt ships (DSB)
Length	164.8 metres	170.2 metres	152.0 metres
Width	17.35 metres	23.8 metres	23.0 metres
Tonnage	12,829	10,822	10,607
Rail deck	405 metres (3 tracks)	680 metres (5 tracks)	495 metres (4 tracks)
Access	Bow and stern	Stern	Bow

	Karl Carstens (DB)	Trelle-borg (SJ)	Great Belt ships (DSB)
Car deck	156 cars	133 cars	–
Access	Side	Side	–
Passengers	1,500	800	2,000
Route	Puttgarden to Rodby	Trelleborg to Sassntz	Nyborg to Korsor
Duration	1 hour	4 hours	1 hour

Even larger train ferry tonnage has been provided for the Helsingborg-Copenhagen service started jointly by Danish and Swedish Railways in 1986, the former organization converting an existing trailer ferry to run as *Trekroner* while SJ built the new 13,000 ton *Oresund*. These ships are used exclusively for freight wagons, and through passenger coaches between Denmark and Sweden still cross the Oresund on the small ferries maintaining the Helsingor-Helsingborg shuttle service.

Dronning Ingrid, one of the trio of Danish State Railways train ferries in use on the Great Belt service between Nyborg and Korsor (Author).

Above *One of the largest pair of vessels ever built for Danish State Railways,* Peder Paars *makes a cautious stern approach to Kalundborg in August 1986* (Author).

Below Silvia Regina *surrounded by ice in Helsinki's South Harbour in March 1985* (Author).

Above left Finlandia *close to Stockholm after an overnight crossing from Helsinki* (Anders Ahlerup).

Left Svea *in comparatively open water during a first summer on the Silja Line Stockholm–Turku service* (Anders Ahlerup).

Below left *A stern view of* Wellamo *leaving Turku, which gives a good impression of the sheer size of the Silja Line giant* (Author).

Above Viking Sally *at speed in the Stockholm archipelago* (Anders Ahlerup).

Below *The world's largest ferry,* Mariella, *moving astern out of Helsinki's South Harbour in June 1986* (Author).

Above   *Arriving at Stockholm:* Olympia *in-bound from Helsinki, soon after joining sister* Mariella *on the Helsinki service* (Anders Ahlerup).

Below   *First purpose-built cruise-ferry introduced for the 24-hour Stockholm–Mariehamn trade was* Birka Princess, *outward bound here from the Swedish capital in June 1986* (Anders Ahlerup).

Chapter 5

The Baltic phenomenon

Without a shadow of doubt the Baltic has seen more dramatic developments over the past thirty years than any other areas of major ferry activity and this remarkable expansion in traffic between Finland and Sweden has centred on the roughly parallel routes linking the respective capital cities, Helsinki and Stockholm, as well as from Turku and Naantali in Finland via the Aland Islands to Stockholm or Kapellskar. Passenger connections between the countries have a history going back to the earliest days of steam navigation yet not until 1959 were serious attempts made to establish roll-on/roll-off services and a further three years passed before the appearance of the first purpose-built tonnage with bow and stern doors and drive-through facilities to handle freight vehicles as well as private cars.

Not much more than two decades later the five largest ferries so far constructed figure in this traffic and by the early 1990s six more huge ferries will have been brought into commission, two of the most recently ordered measuring a staggering 50,000 tons. All of these ships run in the colours of Viking Line or its competitor Silja Line, each organization embracing Swedish and Finnish interests but having very different origins and, until quite recent times, less conflicting commercial objectives. In either case the title represented the marketing spearhead of separate groups of companies whose ships adopted corporate colours and maintained fully-integrated schedules under the respective banners. This still applies for Viking Line but since 1985 there has been a change of responsibilities within the rival operation and the em-

phasis switched increasingly away from the companies providing the ships to Silja Line itself.

The colossal investment in fresh tonnage has been rewarded by ever-increasing business and although it is already estimated that the equivalent of the entire population of Finland has to make at least one crossing a year to produce present figures, the companies are convinced there is potential for still further growth with the ferries and their incredibly high standard of onboard accommodation providing as much a social and recreational amenity as pure transportation.

Even in the depths of winter the ferries continue to plough through the Baltic ice and, despite the sub-zero temperatures, consistently high occupancy levels are maintained, a factor which becomes even more remarkable when it is remembered that Silja Line and Viking Line match one another sailing for sailing on the main Helsinki and Turku routes. Red-hulled Viking ships and their white-painted Silja counterparts depart from either side more or less simultaneously and cross in procession.

Against this curious background Silja Line passengers totals topped two million for the first time in 1986 to complete a period of incredible growth — just 277,000 passengers travelling in 1959 with the one million milestone not achieved until the mid-1960s. Viking Line's performance stands at well over three million passengers annually as they have an additional route, Kapellskar-Aland-Naantali which experiences no competition.

Helsinki can justly claim to be among the ferry capitals of the world with a string of the largest vessels making regular calls. In this typical teatime scene Silvia Regina *(right) is departing for Stockholm to be followed by* Mariella *while* Finnjet *prepares for an early evening sailing to Travemunde (Edwin Wilmshurst).*

Oy Silja Line A/B (Finska Angfartygs A/B (EFFOA) and Johnson Line, Stockholm)

At one stage a consortium of four companies, Silja Line has been an equal partnership between Finland Steamship Company (EFFOA) and Johnson Line of Sweden since 1981. Founded in 1893 and then known as FAA, the Finnish concern first entered into co-operation with Bore Steamship Company of Turku as long ago as 1904 and a new agreement, also including Svea Line of Stockholm, was formulated in 1918. The three companies continued to work successfully although it was the early 1950s before the results of a post-war rebuilding programme were seen and then the trio of vessels introduced were conventional passenger steamers with space for only 25 cars which had to be loaded by crane.

Before long these ships, one for each company, were hard pressed to meet traffic demands and with the time thought to be right for the introduction of car ferries, a jointly-owned subsidiary the Silja Shipping Company came into existence in 1957. A first ro-ro passenger ship was ordered in 1959 and delivered as *Skandia* two years later. It was joined on a fast route from Turku via Aland to Norrtalje by a sister ship, *Nordia*, in 1962.

The original passenger services from Stockholm to Turku and Helsinki continued but a further trio of vessels introduced between 1960 and 1964 still had only small decks capable of taking between 50 and 70 cars driven aboard through side doors. However, all future new ships were car ferries and a fresh basic agreement which came into force in 1970 brought more intensive co-operation between the companies and converted Silja Line into a traffic co-ordinating and marketing unit. One early result was the introduction of the now famous Silja seal's head emblem.

Until the dawn of the 1970s the Helsinki service was withdrawn in the winter but there was a re-organization following the introduction of a pair of French-built ferries to start year-round sailings in 1972. Growth was such that, yet again, these vessels were struggling to cope within a couple of years and a further generation of larger units appeared in 1975. A year later the traditional passenger services from historic Skeppsbron quay in Stockholm were withdrawn and Silja, deciding that the best results could be obtained from running larger ships on fewer routes, concentrated their efforts entirely on Stockholm-Helsinki and Stockholm-Turku passenger and vehicle services.

At the end of the decade Bore Line withdrew from passenger shipping to concentrate on cargo activities leaving Silja then owned equally by EFFOA and Svea. A further major change transpired in 1981 when Svea closed down its shipping operation and was converted into a real estate company. Svea was replaced in the consortium by Johnson Line of Stockholm. EFFOA's own fleet was increased in June 1986 when Finnjet Line and its stylish gas-turbine-powered ferry *Finnjet* was purchased from Enso Gutzeit. Then, early in 1987, EFFOA and Johnson Line announced that they had secured a majority holding in the Aland shipping company and Viking Line consortium founder members Rederi A/B Sally who had left the Viking group in October 1987. During the same month EFFOA ordered from Wartsila, Turku, a ferry of 50,000 tons which, when completed in 1990, will bring even more luxurious standards to the Stockholm-Helsinki route. Johnson Line are expected to take up an option to commission a sister ship in 1991.

There was still a very traditional look to Baltic passenger services at the beginning of the 1970s as shown by this 1971 Stockholm view with the steamers Svea Jarl *and* Bore *alongside the historic Skeppsbron quay. Remarkably, both ships are still in operation,* Svea Jarl, *now with diesel propulsion, making 24 hour cruises from the Swedish capital to Mariehamn as Viking Line's* Apollo III, *while* Bore, *after several changes of ownership and travels as far as the Mediterranean, was bought in 1987 to commence cruises as* Kristina Regina. *New diesel engines replace the steam plant but the original twin funnels are retained* (Anders Ahlerup).

Finlandia/Silvia Regina

Owner Finland Steamship Company (EFFOA)/Johnson Line of Stockholm. **Flag** Finland/Sweden. **Operator** Silja Line. **Route** Stockholm-Helsinki. **Built** Wartsila, Turku, in 1981. **Gross tonnage** 25,678/25,905. **Net tonnage** 14,070. **Length** 166.1 m. **Width** 28.4 m. **Draught** 6.7 m. **Machinery** 4 Pielstick diesels of 22,948 hp. **Speed** 22 knots. **Passengers** 2,000. **Cabin berths** 1,666. **Vehicle capacity** 450 cars. **Vehicle access** Bow and stern.

Despite investing in the 1975 series of French-built 12,000 tonners for the booming Helsinki-Stockholm connection, Silja was again experiencing capacity problems within a comparatively short time and this factor, together with orders for a pair of major ferries for Viking Line's rival service, led to construction of what were the Finland-Sweden trade's most outstanding vessels to date and, at that time, the world's largest ferries. The order went to the Wartsila Turku Yard, reviving ties established a decade before when Wartsila's Helsinki arm delivered the earliest Silja car ferries.

First to be laid down was the vessel to EFFOA's account and it was named *Finlandia* by the country's first lady, Mrs Tellervo Koivisto, on 30 March 1981, going into service the very next day. The sister ship for Svea Line was named *Silvia Regina* by Queen Silvia of Sweden in a ceremony on 28 April also attended by King Carl Gustav and the president of Finland, Urho

Above   Finlandia *leaving Stockholm on her maiden voyage to Helsinki on 3 April 1981* (Anders Ahlerup).

Below   *A couple of years on and* Finlandia *appears against the backdrop of Helsinki with the effects of surgery on the bows clearly apparent* (Silja Line).

Kekkonen. This vessel joined *Finlandia* in service with a maiden sailing on 12 June 1981.

At 25,678 grt the newcomers displaced another regular user of Helsinki, Enso Gutzeit's 24,065 grt *Finnjet*, from its place at the head of the world's 'largest ferries' list although the latter remains the longest ferry and, since the spring of 1986, has been running in Silja colours following purchase by EFFOA. The only obvious difference in appearance between *Finlandia* and *Silvia Regina* is their funnels, the former carrying EFFOA's two white stripes on a black background while *Silvia Regina* briefly wore the white initial 'S' of Svea Line before it was replaced by Johnson Line's yellow star on a blue band.

The style and scale of the main public rooms located on the uppermost deck is the absorbing feature of the two ships which have 1,601 berths in 647 cabins all with *en suite* facilities on four lower decks, plus one small couchette area. The main Maxim's *à la carte* restaurant, situated forward, seats 479 and fronts a dance floor, with a further 491 seats in a terrace restaurant above, where Scandinavian cold table fare is offered. There is an additional grill restaurant and a taverna, plus a conference suite which, following provision of a new auditorium on Deck 8, now handles up to 600 delegates per ship.

Although acquitting themselves well in the ice of a first winter, *Finlandia* and *Silvia Regina* were less at home in the Baltic's autumn gales and quite extensive surgery was carried out on the bows to improve sea keeping qualities when the sisters went back in turn to Wartsila in the spring of 1982. The work had the desired operational result yet rather spoiled the line of the hull, the extra sheer forward leaving the ships looking for all the world as if a giant slice had been chiselled away!

Unlike the Turku route where there is very little scope for full speed running, the Helsinki-Stockholm run is largely open sea and the ships have sufficient reserves of power to make a more southerly sweep, if necessary, when ice conditions prevail. Departure from either side is at 18.00 with arrival next day at 09.00 and as a lot of round trip passengers are carried, the ships are never totally deserted during lay-overs in port.

Spectacular increases in passenger levels were recorded in the first year of the Silja ships and even in 1986 when Viking Line had both their larger new buildings on stream, the

Finlandia and *Silvia Regina* retained their share of the business. Although the Silja partners talked of providing 200 additional berths by lengthening the two ships to 198 metres, this was dropped in favour of a programme of internal rebuilding which commenced in the autumn of 1987 with completion during spring 1988 dry-docking. Apart from general refurbishment, main changes were replacement of the previous children's play area and lobby shop on the fourth deck by a lounge with rest chairs while other features are a larger 'Children's World,' a 200 seat music bar with fine views aft, an additional grill restaurant, a new cafeteria and the creation of a special gourmet section seating 40 in the main à la carte restaurant.

At the end of October 1987 EFFOA ordered a 50,000 ton ferry for introduction on the Helsinki run in 1990 and two months later the sale of *Finlandia* to DFDS, with delivery when the new unit comes into service, was confirmed. Capital for a new building was raised in the same way through an advance sale of *Wellamo* (now *Dana Gloria*) to DFDS in 1980.

Svea/Wellamo

Owner Johnson Line of Stockholm/Finland Steamship Company (EFFOA). **Flag** Sweden/Finland. **Operator** Silja Line. **Route** Stockholm-Mariehamn-Turku. **Built** Wartsila, Helsinki, 1985/1986. **Gross tonnage** 33,830. **Net tonnage** 17,750. **Length** 168 m. **Width** 27.6 m. **Draught** 6.5 m. **Machinery** 4 Wartsila diesels of 26,400 hp. **Speed** 22 knots. **Passengers** 2,000. **Cabin berths** 1,803. **Vehicle capacity** 400 cars. **Vehicle access** Bow, stern and side.

Once *Finlandia* and *Silvia Regina* were established and attracting hugely increased passenger numbers the Silja companies set about providing similar standards on the Turku run. It was not as simple as producing carbon copies of the Helsinki twins, as vessels on the shorter Turku crossing are able to make a full round trip in 24 hours with day departures in either direction calling at Mariehamn in the Aland Islands before direct overnight sailings from Stockholm to Turku or vice-versa. Thus the first major ships specifically designed for the Turku trade for over a decade needed to be able to cater for large numbers of passengers on day trips as well as having cabins and night club style ambience for the evening departures.

Unlike the Helsinki-Stockholm ships with their lengthy spells in port, the pair of 2,000 passenger units ordered from Wartsila, Helsinki

Left *Even the worst of the Baltic winter only rarely disrupts ferry services and* Finlandia *ploughs a straight furrow through the pack ice en-route for Helsinki.* **Inset:** *Sister ship* Silvia Regina, *equally at home amid the sheet ice near the Finnish capital. Note the vessel's bow visor still carrying the houseflag of the original owners Svea Line (Silja Line).*

had to be capable of being turned around in as little as an hour and a maximum of two. The containerized system for catering and bar supplies, already fitted to *Finlandia* and *Silvia Regina*, was repeated, with all waste being off-loaded in a container by the ship's own gantry crane at the terminal port before fresh supplies are hoisted onboard and taken by a special lift direct to the kitchen area.

The first ship, yard number 470, originally ordered by EFFOA, was transferred to Johnson Line ownership whilst fitting out and undertook trials in February 1985. The ship was named *Svea* by celebrated Swedish singer Birgit Nilsson on 7 May before being officially handed over in a ceremony held at sea off the Finnish coast. *Svea* later continued to Stockholm and then to Turku with invited guests and finally entered service on 13 May. The sister ship was floated out of the covered building dock as early as March 1985 but trials were delayed until November because, for accounting reasons, EFFOA did not want to take delivery until the beginning of the following year.

Svea's introduction in 1985 was largely responsible for a 30 per cent increase in business in and out of Turku and there was further major progress in 1986 when *Wellamo* completed the two ship line-up for one of the world's most spectactular scheduled passages through the thousands of islands of the Stockholm Archipelago and Aland Sea. The route is often said to add an extra dimension to this travel experience and in addition to a larger amount of deck space than in many modern ferries, the ships have their main restaurants situated to give panoramic views forward or over the stern.

The terrace concept of the Helsinki ships is repeated but in *Svea* and *Wellamo* a 275-seat

The classic Aland archipelago view of a brand new Svea *gliding through mirrored waters close to Turku* (Arvo Salminen).

Above   *On the Swedish side closer to Stockholm the surroundings can be just as idyllic with* Svea *reflecting the breakfast time sun when outward bound for Turku in June 1986* (Author).

Below   Svea's *Finnish flag sister* Wellamo, *seen on sea trials, was completed towards the end of 1985 but for accounting purposes EFFOA did not take delivery until 1 January 1986* (Wartsila, Helsinki).

Sky Bar complete with gurgling fountains is at the upper level. There is a 480 seat *à la carte* restaurant below which includes a dance floor, while on the same deck aft, a further 306 seats are available in a buffet restaurant and each ship also has an additional cafeteria and gourmet dining room.

The extensive conference facilities on board even boast their own sauna unit and share the top passenger deck with a vast duty free shopping area, the latter emphasizing the importance of this form of revenue to all Baltic ferry companies. Silja'a slightly 'up market' image and higher fares have tended not to attract the younger element though this is changing and both ships have impressive disco clubs conveniently out of earshot at the very lowest level and actually beneath the smart main sauna and swimming pools.

Quite extensive shore work was necessary before the *Svea* and *Wellamo* entered service. A new berth and improvements to the terminal were necessary at Turku; a new berth was built too at Mariehamn — where the calls in either direction last precisely ten minutes — and a further new berth was constructed at Vartan Terminal in Stockholm. Loading is via stern ramps at the Swedish end and apart from space for 350 cars on the main and platform decks, another forty cars are accommodated in a separate upper garage loaded from fixed inclined ramps on the quays which connect with a starboard side door.

New Buildings (2)
Owner Finland Steamship Co (EFFOA)/Johnson Line of Stockholm. **Flag** Finland/Sweden. **Operator** Silja Line. **Route** Helsinki-Stockholm. **Built** Ordered from Wartsila, Turku, for delivery in 1990 (EFFOA) and optional, 1991 (Johnson Line). **Gross tonnage** ca 50,000. **Net tonnage** Not available. **Length** 200 m. **Width** 31.5 m. **Draught** 6.8 m. **Machinery** 4 diesels of 43,000 hp. **Speed** 22 knots. **Passengers** 2,500. **Cabin berths** 2,500. **Vehicle capacity** 450 cars. **Vehicle access** Bow, stern and side.

Silja Line's super-ferries for the 1990s will not carry any more passengers or vehicles than their 1980s predecessors but look set to herald the start of a fresh Baltic era as far as the quality and style of accommodation and customer service is concerned. EFFOA signed a contract on 26 October 1987 for Wartsila Marine Industries to construct the world's first 50,000 ton passenger ferry with delivery due in the spring of 1990 and

partners Johnson Line are expected to exercise their option for a sister ship to be completed approximately a year later.

To be built at Wartsila's Turku yard, the new generation ships are literally luxury hotels of a standard never before seen afloat. The most striking feature will be a restaurant, three stories high, with views forward through a single huge panaromic window. Current Silja Line ships have restaurants two decks in height but these are nothing by comparison with what will be seen in the new vessels!

Silja managing director Ralf Sandstrom says the aim is to increase leisure and travel possibilities open to active people but stresses that the ships will be designed to meet all environmental protection demands including everything from waste disposal to wave formation and exhaust emissions.

There will be cabin berths for all 2,500 passengers and space on the vehicle decks for up to 450 cars or 60 trailers. To ease the changeover to the new ferries (which will cost over 7 billion FIM each) Silja's existing Helsinki-Stockholm ferries *Finlandia* and *Silvia Regina* were thoroughly modernized in the winter of 1987/88 with most of the emphasis on improvements to the restaurant deck. As mentioned earlier, *Finlandia* has already been sold to DFDS Seaways and will be handed over when the first new ship enters service.

Finnjet
Owner Finland Steamship Co (EFFOA). **Flag** Finland. **Operator** Finnjet Silja Line. **Route** Helsinki-Travemunde. **Built** Wartsila, Helsinki, in 1977. **Gross tonnage** 24,065. **Net tonnage** 10,786. **Length** 212.8 m. **Width** 25.4 m. **Draught** 7.2 m. **Machinery** 2 Pratt & Whitney gas turbines of 75,000 hp and 2 Wartsila diesels of 15,500 hp. **Speed** 31 knots, 20 knots. **Passengers** 1,790. **Cabin berths** 1,790. **Vehicle capacity** 374 cars. **Vehicle access** Bow and stern.

Ferry connections between Germany and Finland, although well established and served by modern ferries, took as much as two days for the 660 nautical mile passage until the appearance in 1977 of *Finnjet*, a vessel that remains one of the most advanced ever constructed. Designed to halve the travelling time between Helsinki and Travemunde, *Finnjet* was the first passenger and vehicle ferry to exceed 20,000 tons and, still the longest and fastest in its class, was virtually re-launched from a sales angle following a major refurbish-

Above *Still the world's fastest ferry,* Finnjet *makes an awesome sight storming across the Baltic at over 30 knots powered by a pair of Pratt and Whitney gas turbines* (Wartsila, Helsinki).

ment early in 1986 and then purchase later in the year by EFFOA.

The idea of a high-speed Baltic service by a ferry of real distinction was conceived by Finnish shipowner and industrialist Enso Gutzeit, the man who already maintained sea connections with Germany through his Finnlines sailings, before also developing Vaasanlaivat's Finland-Sweden links across the Gulf of Bothnia. Apart from the potential for increased wheeled freight traffic to Finland from Northern Europe, the enormous scope for tourist business out of Germany provided an irresistible challenge for Gutzeit.

Ordered from Wartsila, Helsinki, *Finnjet* really established the yard as a force in the construction of passenger ships and to achieve the service speed of 30.5 knots necessary for 22½-hour crossings during the summer peak, a marine adaption of the type of Pratt and Whitney gas turbines used to power widebodied DC10 aircraft was chosen, the two units producing 75,000 hp and being able to accelerate the ship to top speed in under four minutes from a complete standstill while still having sufficient reserves of power to deal with

winter ice.

Able to take 1,532 passengers, all berthed, and up to 350 cars, *Finnjet* entered service in May 1977 and completed 209 round trips in its first twelve months including a less intensive winter schedule. The vessel achieved average loadings in excess of 700 and total carryings of 144,497 — a figure nearly double that of the previous year when Finnlines maintained sailings with a pair of more ordinary ferries!

But it was not all plain sailing. The recession in Europe halted the upward surge in passenger levels, competition for freight traffic intensified and *Finnjet* was more vulnerable than conventionally powered ferries to increases in fuel costs. Some positive action was needed and late in 1981 Gutzeit sent the ship to Amsterdam where areas of the main car deck were sacrificed to provide space for a separate set of diesel engines for use out of the main season. Two Wartsila units producing 15,500 hp were fitted to drive the existing twin screws and give *Finnjet* an 18–20 knot capability on a 38-hour offpeak sailing schedule covering two weekly round trips and usually lasting from the middle of August until early the following June. At the

Another view of Finnjet *looking impressive in its new Silja Line colour scheme after repainting in the spring of 1987* (Finnjet Silja Line).

height of the summer *Finnjet* uses the gas turbines to make three return sailings each week and is once again running close to capacity with a very high level of support from Germany.

Internally, *Finnjet* showed a departure from previous Baltic styling with a vertical division of principal passenger decks for cabin accommodation to be situated forward and public rooms aft. The better grade cabins are extremely spacious and during the 1986 refit 28 luxury double cabins in a new 'Commodore Class' category were added together with their own day lounge and sauna unit. At the same time the main entertainment deck was completely redesigned with the dance saloon and bar enlarged, a new *à la carte* restaurant and improved shopping facilities in the form of a series of boutiques introduced.

Although a large scale publicity campaign supported what was advertised from early in 1986 as the 'new' *Finnjet*, renewed speculation arose when it was revealed that DFDS had put in a bid to secure the ship for its Copenhagen-Oslo service. Then EFFOA announced they had bought both vessel and the Finnjet Line operation from Gutzeit with effect from the beginning of June. No changes were made to the pattern of sailings and a similar programme followed in 1987 marketed as Finnjet Silja Line, the *Finnjet* itself emerging from a nine-day April dry docking repainted white with the black and white striped funnel of EFFOA and Silja's seal's head emblem and logo on the hull.

Viking Line (Rederi A/B Sally, Mariehamn; SF Line, Mariehamn; Rederi A/B Slite, Stockholm)

Thirty years ago the main ferry routes between Sweden and Finland looked so secure in the control of the co-operating trio of FAA, Bore Line and Svea Line that serious doubts would have been expressed about the sanity of anyone rash enough to try to compete. Yet within a week at the beginning of 1959 two quite independent rival operations got underway, one started by a couple of Aland sea captains using a 35-year-old former British cross-Channel steamer, and the other on the initiative of a Swedish ship owner with a converted cargo boat. Each concern prospered and laid the foundations of Viking Line, the most influential Baltic ferry force during the past two decades.

Captain Gunnar Eklund and close friend Cap-

Three ships that helped revolutionize Baltic ferry services almost thirty years ago. Former Southern Railways steamer Dinard *began running as* Viking *on the same day in 1959 as converted cargo boat* Slite *was put into operation. Four years later another British veteran,* Brittany, *was introduced as* Alandsfarjan *and is pictured at Graddo dressed overall for the first trip* (Viking Line).

tain Henning Rundberg were convinced car ferries running on the shortest and most direct routes between ports in Stockholm's outer archipelago and Finland could be utilized fully for two round trips a day and be viable even with low passenger and vehicle fares. They paid £30,000 for the former Southern Railway overnight ferry *Dinard*, rebuilt to carry 70 cars and 350 passengers on the Dover-Boulogne route following Second World War service as a hospital ship at Dunkirk, in the Mediterranean and for the Normandy landings. Car capacity was increased slightly during a refit in Denmark at Aalborg and it was as *Viking* that the twin-funnelled veteran began running between Graddo and Korpo on 1 June 1959.

Five days later the 499-ton motor ship *Slite* commenced twice daily sailings from Mariehamn to Simpnas in Sweden and Carl-Bertil Myrsten's Rederi AB Slite was born, if just a little chaotically — the ship ran aground near Simpnas during the maiden sailing, the cafeteria ran out of food and there was also insufficient crockery to go round! But by the end of that first summer Viking Line and Slite had more than silenced the sceptics, carrying a total of 88,000 passengers, 13,000 cars and, significantly, 600 lorries and 60 coaches between them. Car ferries were definitely on the Aland sea to stay!

A split between the original Viking Line partners in 1963 resulted in Gunnar Eklund forming Alandsfarjan AB and starting a Mariehamn-Graddo route with another former Southern Railway vessel, the Channel Islands steamer *Brittany* of 1933 which was converted to carry 30 cars and given the name *Alandsfarjan*. The other companies continued as before and the first car ferry built to Scandinavian ice class for year round operation was Slite's *Apollo*, delivered in 1963. When consideration was be-

ing given to its hull colours one of the owner's relatives found a unique way of solving the problem by producing her lipstick!

First hint of co-operation came in 1965 when Viking Line and Slite began running a joint service from Kapellskar via Aland to Parainen in Finland using *Viking* and *Apollo*. Alandsfarjan joined them in 1966 when Viking Line was transformed into a marketing company to coordinate sales, bookings, timetables and other matters. The corporate image was extended to the ships which were all given the dark red hulls adopted by Slite a couple of years earlier. The original Viking Line, which became Rederi AB Solstad, was soon bought out by Rederi AB Sally. The consortium's present shape was completed in 1969 when Alandsfarjan changed its name to SF Line.

The 1970s saw no fewer than a dozen major ferries put into operation, all but one purpose built and including a series of six smaller vessels from a single yard, the Meyer Werft at Papenburg in West Germany. Naturally, services expanded and in addition to the early direct route

Viking Line companies soon moved away from using secondhand tonnage and Viking 1 *was among the first of a series of no fewer than six ferries built in Germany by the Meyer Yard at Papenburg between 1970 and 1975. They were the springboard for expansion but quickly became overtaken by pace of traffic growth and* Viking 1 *was the last of the half dozen still in the fleet when sold in 1983 (Viking Line).*

for which Naantali became the Finnish terminal, a Stockholm-Mariehamn-Turku run began in direct opposition to Silja Line in 1973 and a year later Viking extended the competition to Stockholm-Helsinki but stuck to its original philosophy of aiming for mass support by offering lower fares.

SF Line's *Turella* became Viking's first ship to exceed 10,000 tons in June 1979 with a sister vessel *Rosella* following a year later, by which time Slite had stolen the honours with the 11,653 ton *Diana II*. Sally became the dominant partners at this time and in little more than two months during the summer of 1980 took delivery of three large new ferries, the luxurious 13,878 ton *Viking Saga* and *Viking Song* for the Helsinki service and, even larger at 15,500 tons, *Viking Sally*, for the Turku route.

Unlike the other partners who stuck exclusively to ferries, Sally developed wider shipping interests. The bought Enso Gutzeit's Vaasanlaivat operation with routes across the Gulf of Bothnia from Vaasa to both Sundsvall and Umea; established an English Channel outpost with the Sally Line service from Ramsgate to Dunkirk — and instigated major developments of Ramsgate as a ferry port. They also became involved in Caribbean cruising and developed extensive bulk carrier interests. Difficulties with deep sea operations reduced their influence within the Viking group and SF and Slite took over the Helsinki service after producing the world's largest ferries, the outstanding *Mariella* in 1985 and *Olympia* a year later.

SF next set about countering Silja Line's new Turku route tonnage with orders for two more ships of over 30,000 tons from builders in Yugoslavia for delivery early in 1988 and 1989 respectively and then, in March 1987, it was the Slite Company's turn to announce the order of a 35,000 ton ferry from Wartsila with an option for a sister ship. SF Line also went back to basics, buying the small former English Channel ferry *Tiger* from Townsend Thoresen for use on a summer shuttle between Kapellskar and Mariehamn as *Alandsfarjan*, reviving a historic name also used for different ships chartered to fulfil a similar peak season role in previous years. But *Alandsfarjan*, at less than 5,000 tons and with no cabins or ice classification, is still quite a contrast to SF's 37,799 ton flagship, *Mariella*.

The *Alandsfarjan* increased Viking's fleet to seven ships for 1987 summer sailings, four owned by SF Line, two provided by Slite and just one for Sally, a company by then entirely owned by the Silja Line partners EFFOA and Johnson Line with a minority holding by Finnish banking interests. However, it was stressed that the takeover would not affect the day-to-day running of the Viking or Silja groups and that Sally's Vaasa services and foreign interests would be maintained. But SF Line and Slite were less than happy with the new set-up which threatened to give major competitor Silja a foothold in the Viking camp, and took legal steps to safeguard their position. By the autumn of 1987 matters had been resolved, Sally leaving the Viking consortium completely, with their single remaining ship chartered by Slite.

Viking Sally

Owner Rederi AB Sally. **Flag** Finnish. **Operator** Viking Line. **Route** Stockholm-Mariehamn-Turku. **Built** Jos L Meyer of Papenburg, in 1980. **Gross tonnage** 15,567. **Net tonnage** 8,372. **Length** 155.4 m. **Width** 24.2 m. **Draught** 5.5 m. **Machinery** 4 Man diesels of 17,652 hp. **Speed** 21.2 knots. **Passengers** 2,000. **Cabin berths** 1,168. **Vehicle capacity** 460 cars. **Vehicle access** Bow and stern.

The half dozen ferries delivered by Jos L. Meyer of Papenburg between 1970 and 1974 provided the backbone of Viking Line's network of services for almost a decade and, in all, no fewer than nine similar ships were built with a further trio going to Mexican owners. Although Meyer produced a larger one-off vessel, Slite's *Diana II*, which had some similarities to the earlier sisters, the German yard's real hopes for a replacement series were pinned on a much more advanced unit ordered by SF Line for delivery in 1980. SF later decided it had sufficient tonnage and cancelled and, while Sally took over, there were no follow-on orders. The single ship was named *Viking Sally* by Mrs Anna Johansson, wife of the company's managing director on 26 April 1980, delivered on 29 June and brought into service on 5 July.

Viking Sally, then the biggest ferry running between Finland and Sweden, brought a major boost in terms of both quality and capacity to Stockholm-Mariehamn-Turku sailings yet, despite being larger, it always seemed slightly overshadowed by the Sally sisters introduced on the more prestigious Helsinki route in the same summer. *Viking Sally*, with room for 2,000 passengers and berths for a little over half this figure on night crossings, was the first Viking ship on the Turku route with such refinements as an indoor swimming pool and the main service areas are well laid-out on three decks aft of the cabins.

To ensure revenue was shared evenly, ships on the Turku and Naantali routes were switched from time to time and this brought *Viking Sally* on to the Kapellskar-Mariehamn-Naantali circuit from the beginning of June 1982, but it was back on the Stockholm-Turku run by the following year when Viking celebrated its 25th anniversary.

Despite the Sally company's fluctuating fortunes, *Viking Sally* has continued covering the demanding Turku schedules exclusively and has always enjoyed a reputation for being smartly operated. Since late April 1986 she has been Sally's only ship running in Viking colours

Above   *Ordered by SF Line and later completed for Rederi Sally,* Viking Sally *represented the Meyer super-ferry concept but the yard's hopes of follow-on orders as replacements for the 1970s series came to nothing* (Anders Ahlerup).

Below   Viking Sally *at Turku in 1986, the last Sally ship running in Viking services. The 'duck-tail' at the stern, designed to reduce wash and improve operating efficiency in the Stockholm archipelago and Åland sea, can be clearly identified* (Author).

but achieved a career milestone in August 1987 when carrying her seven millionth passenger. By the end of the following October Sally had left the Viking group and *Viking Sally* had been chartered by Rederi Slite to continue on the Turku run for 18 months until the first of their new buildings from Wartsila is ready. After that *Viking Sally* could be refitted to take over Sally's Helsinki-based cruise operation releasing the rebuilt *Sally Albatross* for deployment elsewhere and most probably in the Caribbean.

Mariella/Olympia

Owner SF Line Mariehamn/Rederi AB Slite. **Flag** Finland/Sweden. **Operator** Viking Line. **Route** Stockholm-Helsinki. **Built** Wartsila, Turku, in 1985/1986. **Gross tonnage** 37,779. **Net tonnage** 23,644. **Length** 177 m. **Width** 28.4 m. **Draught** 6.5 m. **Machinery** 4 Pielstick diesels of 31,280 hp. **Speed** 22 knots. **Passengers** 2,500. **Cabin berths** 2,447. **Vehicle capacity** 580 cars. **Vehicle access** Bow and stern.

Viking Line's appearance on the Helsinki-Stockholm run in 1973 was due entirely to the efforts of Sally whose partners agreed to them having sole operating rights for a period of ten years. It quickly became a major money spinner and the success story continued when, in 1980, Sally commissioned *Viking Saga* and *Viking Song*, the most impressive ships yet seen on a Baltic overnight service. But when Silja Line regained the initiative with their huge 1981 sisters *Silvia Regina* and *Finlandia*, Sally did not have the resources to build again and with the old agreement having run its course SF Line and Slite moved into the Helsinki business in dramatic fashion, placing orders in December 1983 for the world's largest ferries.

The keel of the first of the pair was laid down for SF Line at Wartslia's Turku yard in April 1984 and thanks to considerable use of prefabricated construction techniques the ship took to the water just five months later when named *Mariella* by Scandinavian celebrity Carita Blomsterlund. SF Line accepted delivery on 17 May 1985 and *Mariella* went into service next day, replacing *Viking Saga* which was immediately sold to Fred Olsen Lines. In the meantime Slite's ship was taking shape at Turku and was given the name *Olympia* on the last day of August 1985 in a ceremony performed by Miss Elise Myrsten, daughter of Slite's founder Carl-Bertil Myrsten. The new ship joined *Mariella* on 28 May the following year.

Below *The world's largest ferry,* Mariella, *was introduced on the Stockholm-Helsinki service in 1985 and, in the first twelve months of operation, never sailed with less than a thousand passengers on board* (Anders Ahlerup).

Mariella never made a crossing with fewer than 1,000 passengers in her first twelve months in service and demonstrated once again the ability of new Baltic ferries to generate fresh business and maintain the expansion of the market overall. The big Viking ships are vibrant and perhaps even a little brash: they certainly present a contrast to the more restrained style of travel offered by Silja Line. The stunning effect of *Mariella* and *Olympia* hits passengers as soon as they set foot in the huge reception halls with their abundance of marble and brass. One deck higher, all the major public rooms are connected by a bright, wide starboard-side arcade dotted with clusters of seats offering views of the passing scenery through large windows.

The buffet restaurant on each ship can handle 556 passengers at one time and a lot of thought also went into the layout and decoration of a selction of gourmet restaurants amidships. The *Mariella* and her sister take up to 2,500 passengers and there are small numbers of

Left *Mariella* *is big and impressive (*Anders Ahlerup).

Below *Departure time at Helsinki as* Mariella *eases away from her berth at the start of another overnight voyage to Stockholm* (Author).

Olympia departing from Stockholm in August 1986 after joining sister Mariella *on the Helsinki service. Viking Line has long advertised its routes as extensions of the international motorway system, hence the prominently displayed 'E3' symbol on the superstructure* (Anders Ahlerup).

couchettes and rest chairs in addition to the range of 841 cabins offering 2,387 berths including half a dozen opulent suites and a further 25 cabins classified merely as 'de luxe'! With such a huge number of cabins spread over no fewer than five different decks onboard orientation could easily have been a problem but internal direction signs are very effective and easy to follow.

Back in Sally's era on the route Viking began to challenge the Silja hold in such areas as conference traffic and this has been developed significantly in the present ships which have the fore part of Deck 8 devoted to meeting rooms of various sizes opening off a conference centre reception area and a stylish main auditorium seating over 400 that can, if required, be divided into two completely independent halls.

Mariella and *Olympia* take over 60 lorries and 580 cars on main and platform vehicle decks with bow loading at Stockholm and via the double width stern ramps in Helsinki's South Harbour where new facilities were provided before the two ships entered service. They are powered by four Wartsila-built Pielstick 12 PC2-6V engines developing 32,280 hp at 520 rpm and driving twin screws with Stromberg alternators — giving a service speed of 22 knots.

These vessels have been a huge success on the Helsinki service and have given Viking an edge over Silja in terms of passenger figures for the first time since the early 1980s. Just what steps will be taken to counter the debut of Silja's even larger vessels from 1990 remains to be seen and, if nothing else, an intensification of the present vigorous advertising campaigns seems certain.

Amorella/New building 2

Owner SF Line of Mariehamn. **Flag** Finland. **Operator** Viking Line. **Route** Stockholm-Mariehamn-Turku. **Built** Bordogradiliste, Split, Yugoslavia, for delivery in 1988/1989. **Gross tonnage** ca 30,000. **Net tonnage** Not available. **Length** 167.7 m. **Width** 27.6 m. **Draught** 6 m. **Machinery** 4 Pielstick diesels of 24,000 hp. **Speed** 21.5 knots. **Passengers** 2,200. **Cabin berths** 2,000. **Vehicle capacity** 640 cars. **Vehicle access** Bow, stern and side.

*Externally the new Baltic ferries for Viking Line partners SF Line (**above**) and Rederi A/B Slite (**below**) have few features in common. SF's first Yugoslavian building,* Amorella, *due to enter service in April 1988 — with a sister ship following in Spring 1989 — is similar in appearance to* Mariella *and* Olympia *delivered in 1985 and 1986. The Slite ships from Wartsila show characteristics of the same yard's Silja Line products* Svea *and* Wellamo *whilst going back to the mid-hull positioning of lifeboats last seen when* Viking Saga *and* Viking Song *were on the Helsinki run. All four vessels will accommodate over 2,000 passengers apiece and interior design is in the hands of Robert Tilburg from whom some features of the Slite sisters are reported to be quite revolutionary (Viking Line).*

Slite new buildings (2)

Owner Rederi AB Slite of Stockholm. **Flag** Sweden. **Operator** Viking Line. **Route** Kapellskar-Mariehamn-Naantali. **Built** Wartsila, Helsinki, for delivery in 1989/1990. **Gross tonnage** ca 35,000. **Net tonnage** Not available. **Length** 175 m. **Width** 29 m. **Draught** 6.3 m. **Machinery** Not available. **Speed** 21 knots. **Passengers** 2,200. **Cabin berths** 1,735. **Vehicle capacity** 2,750 lane metres. **Vehicle access** Bow, stern and side.

Just as Sally pushed forward a decade ago, there now seems no stopping the SF Line and Slite bandwagon and once the new Viking Line tonnage had settled down on the Helsinki route, the Aland-based company ordered a substantial vessel to match Silja Line's new *Svea* and *Wellamo* on the Stockholm-Turku run. Later it was announced that an option for a sister ship was being taken up with deliveries due in time for the summer peak of 1988 and 1989 respectively. In March 1987 Slite followed with their own order for a 35,000 ton vessel to be constructed by Wartsila for the Turku or the Kapellskar-Mariehamn-Naantali run and later an option for a sister ship was confirmed.

The main shock provided by SF was when they ordered not from Wartsila or Valmet in Finland, or any one of a further half dozen interested North European builders, but from the Yugoslavian Bordogradiliste yard in Split, a concern that has never built super–ferries before and has not turned out a passenger ship of any description for over twenty years — but drastically undercut their rivals and still guaranteed compliance with SF Line's delivery dates. Construction of the first ship progressed on schedule and, unusually for Scandinavian owners who do not normally name their vessels until completion, it was launched as *Amorella* during July 1987.

SF's new buildings are 167 metres long and 27.6 metres in width which figures suggest a gross tonnage well in excess of 30,000 and there will be berths for 90 per cent of total passenger complement of 2,200, plus vehicle space for 640 cars and 53 lorries carried on three levels — including an upper deck with separate access via side doors.

Artist's impressions of the new ships for Slite show some resemblance to the Turku-built Sally ships of 1980 with mid-hull positioned lifeboats but a definite switch to the style of giant forward observation windows seen in the Silja Line jumbos. Accommodation design is considerably more far reaching than anything seen previously, even on the Baltic! Many side cabins on the upper decks are to have windows angled to give passengers a forward view whilst a lavish main nightclub towards the stern will actually extend over the sides of the hull on either beam. There will be an additional half deck with side loading exclusively for 150 cars and a total of 2,750 lane metres will be available for vehicles, with bow and stern doors for the main decks. As the vessels are to be used on routes requiring careful navigation through the Stockholm archipelago and the islands of the Aland sea, the hulls are specially designed to minimize wash and suction.

Sally Albatross

Owner Foreningsbanken. **Flag** Finland. **Operator** Oy Sally Line AB. **Route** Cruises from Helsinki. **Built** Wartsila, Turku, Finland, in 1980. **Gross tonnage** 13,879. **Net tonnage** 7,236. **Length** 145.5 m. **Width** 25.2 m. **Draught** 5.5 m. **Machinery** 4 Pielstick diesels of 24,000 hp. **Speed** 21.3 knots. **Passengers** 2,000. **Cabin berths** 1,223. **Vehicle capacity** 500. **Vehicle access** Bow and stern. **Former names** *Viking Saga* (Viking Line 1980–85). **Sister vessel** *Braemar* (Fred Olsen Lines).

Although no longer operating as a ferry in the accepted traditional sense, *Sally Albatross* is an example of what can be done with an overnight vessel without making radical changes to internal arrangements or even moving far from a previous sphere of operation. Built as *Viking Saga* for Rederi Sally and placed with sister *Viking Song* on the Viking Line service between Helsinki and Stockholm, the two ships lifted Baltic standards to a new level and in many respects their eventual replacements *Mariella* and *Olympia* provided only similar accommodation for greater numbers on a rather more grandiose scale.

Viking Saga, named in March 1980 and delivered by Wartsila, Turku, late in June of the same year, was sold by Sally in June 1982 to Finsk Foretagsfinans, a Helsinki finance company, and leased back immediately. After sharing the service with *Mariella* from May 1985 there seemed a possibility at one stage that Sally would keep the ship on the Stockholm run making day crossings, but they decided instead to start a new Helsinki-based cruise company offering, in the main, 24-hour cruises from Helsinki into the Baltic and Gulf of Finland.

Released by the delivery of *Olympia*, *Viking Saga* was put through a £1 million refurbish-

Above   *It is interesting to compare* Mariella *and* Olympia *with* Viking Saga *which represents the previous generation of Stockholm–Helsinki ferries and was used on the route from 1980 until May 1985* (Anders Ahlerup).

Below   *When* Viking Saga *was displaced by the huge* Olympia, *her owners set up a new operation to use the ship on 24-hour cruises from Helsinki as* Sally Albatross. *The vessel is seen here entering the South Harbour soon after the service started in May 1986* (Author).

ment before a cruising debut as *Sally Albatross* and with destinations usually alternating between Riga and Visby. Public support increased steadily during 1986 with further improvements made during a 1987 refit including provision of an additional bar saloon in front of the funnels. The vessel was sent to Seebeckwerft in Bremerhaven for an even more extensive refit in the opening months of 1988 and while the car carrying capacity is retained, more luxurious cabins suitable for longer cruises have been fitted, which suggests that *Sally Albatross* might ultimately leave the Baltic for the lucrative American market in which Sally already has an interest through a subsidiary company.

Birka Line, Stockholm

Whilst first contact with the Baltic ferry scene as represented by the giants of Viking Line and Silja Line can be mind boggling, there are anomalies, not least the booming trade in 24-hour cruises from Stockholm to Mariehamn that has grown through the past two decades and now boasts specially built tonnage. Most of the ships used have been former ferries of varying degrees of antiquity, and still running with a staunchly loyal clientele are two of the veterans from the final days of Silja Line services from the Swedish capital with conventional ferries.

Birka Line, founded as Alandslinjen in 1971, competed initially for a share of the ordinary ferry traffic before cruises became their sole interest and although the passage to Aland takes no more than six hours in either direction, the ships have to be away from Stockholm for 24 hours to ensure passengers qualify for duty free allowance. Starting with a couple of former DFDS ships, Birka used the Wartsila-built former Finnlines vessel *Finnhansa* as *Prinsessan* with great success before deciding to move into the super-ferry class with a completely new vessel.

Birka Princess

Owner Birka Line. **Flag** Finnish. **Operator** Birka Line. **Route** Stockholm-Mariehamn. **Built** Valmet, Helsinki, in 1986. **Gross tonnage** 21,484. **Net tonnage** 10,537. **Length** 141 m. **Width** 24.7 m. **Draught** 5.6 m. **Machinery** 4 Wartsila diesels of 17,652 hp. **Speed** 20 knots. **Passengers** 1,500. **Cabin berths** 1,100. **Vehicle capacity** 100 cars. **Vehicle access** Starboard side.

Although a ship designed unashamedly for the cruise trade, *Birka Princess* does show just a hint of a ferry ancestory with small vehicle

Although essentially a purpose built cruise ship, Birka Princess *has a small garage for eighty cars loaded through the side port, clearly visible at the stern as the vessel passes Lidingo, bound for Stockholm from Mariehamn in July 1986* (Anders Ahlerup).

decks capable of taking about 100 cars, loaded through an after door on the port side. The order was secured in the face of strong competition by the Valmet Yard at Helsinki and *Birka Princess* was completed in April 1986, just before an amalgamation between the builders and the Helsinki end of the Wartsila operation.

Birka Princess sails year round from the owner's extended Stockholm terminal just around the corner from the historic Skeppsbron, usually departing in the early evening and giving passengers several hours in Mariehamn next morning before the afternoon return trip. Cabins berthing 1,292 passengers all have private facilities and 1,500 can be carried in surroundings which, while attractive, with pastel shades predominating, are rather more restrained than the marble and brass of the Viking Line.

A vigorous publicity campaign pulled no punches in the weeks leading up to the delivery of *Birka Princess*, with a 'Silja luxury at Viking prices' message seemingly on every hoarding, bus and tram in Stockholm. But while Birka are not looking for the traditional Viking Line customers and even discourage under 21's by not serving them in the bars, the ship quickly gained a large following and Birka also joined the big companies in a bid to woo conference and trade customers with a self-contained conference area, including space for presentations and special promotions.

Power is provided by a quartet of Wartsila Vasa diesels and a trial speed of 22 knots was recorded, although in service 18 knots is rarely exceeded and for many of the passages through the Stockholm archipelago strict speed restrictions have to be observed.

Rederiaktiebolget Gotland

After providing services from the Island of Gotland to the Swedish mainland and Oland for an unbroken run of 122 years, Rederi AB Gotland lost operating rights from the end of 1987 despite a long struggle to obtain sanction to continue from the Swedish Transport Council. The main criticisms levelled at the historic company were over the fare structure and actual timing of sailings on the year round run to Gotland's principle town and port Visby from both Nynashamn and Oskarshamn, as well as summer links with a third mainland port, Vastervik, and also to and from Grankullavik on the northern tip of Oland. However, replacement company and shipping newcomers Nord-

strom and Thulin, trading as Gotlandslinjen, are using Gotlandsbolaget's largest ferry *Visby* on charter.

Vessels of quite modest size were adequate for the Gotlandsbolaget services and there was hardly a dramatic increase in tonnages following the introduction of drive-on/off operations. From the early 1970s the 6,642 ton sisters *Gotland* and *Visby*, ordered from Yugoslavia, were used for key services until the company found itself being pushed somewhat reluctantly into the super-ferry era, the Swedish government providing huge subsidies for two ferries of almost 15,000 tons largely to keep the ailing Oresundsvarvet Shipyard at Landskrona in business.

While construction was still in progress Gotlandsbolaget began having second thoughts about the need for two ships with well over 1,100 overnight berths on crossings occupying no more than four or five hours and after the lead ship (*Visby*) was completed late and had a problematic early career, its sister ship, due to have been named *Gotland*, was chartered to Vaasanlaivat before completion and launched as *Wasa Star*. Alas, she fared little better and had a somewhat nomadic existence until bought to run for Larvik Line as *Peter Wessel* between Larvik and Frederikshavn.

Visby

Owner Gotlandsbolaget. **Flag** Swedish. **Operator** Gotlandslinjen. **Route** Nynashamn-Visby. **Built** Oresundvarvet in 1980. **Gross tonnage** 14,932. **Net tonnage** 8,370. **Length** 142.3 m. **Width** 24 m. **Draught** 5.5 m. **Machinery** 4 B & W diesels of 21,476 hp. **Speed** 21 knots. **Passengers** 2,000. **Cabin berths** 926 + 208 couchettes. **Vehicle capacity** 515 cars. **Vehicle access** Bow, stern and side. **Sister vessel** *Peter Wessel* (Larvik Line).

The original contract price for *Visby*, the fifth Gotland ship to carry the name, was SK 165 million which escalated first to SK 210 million and then SK 237 million with government aid to the Landskrona yard probably pushing the final figure close to SK 400 million. Little wonder the venture was soon being described as the biggest gamble in Swedish shipbuilding history and it also failed in the prime objective of securing a long term future for Oresundvarvet. *Visby* was finally delivered five months behind schedule — which cost a further SK 5 million in penalty charges — and for the Gotland company the problems were only just starting.

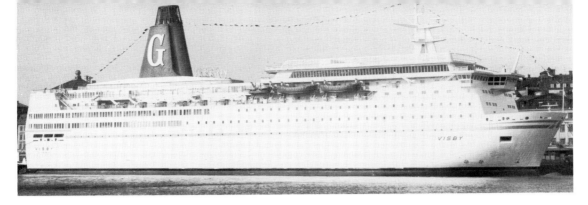

Gotlandsbolaget's Visby *dressed overall for an arrival at Oskarshamn from Visby in July 1982* (Anders Ahlerup).

In deadweight terms *Visby* proved some 800 tons heavier than expected — this increased draught to 5.28 metres and caused all sorts of headaches following a first arrival of *Visby* (on 22 October 1980) where the harbour depth is six metres. Several days of frantic efforts to lighten the ship followed before it entered service, yet after only three weeks on the Nyashamn run the *Visby* started leaking and was sent back to Lanskrona where a fault in a cooling system was discovered and rectified.

Poor Gotlandsbolaget had had enough. When *Visby* returned she was laid-up at Slite to spend the winter as a monument to miscalculation and was not brought back into service until the summer of 1981. By then the company seemed to have decided to make the best of a bad job and smaller units were disposed of: among them was the previous *Visby*, completed in 1972 and renamed *Drotten* in 1980 before the launching of the present ship.

Visby made a first visit to Stockholm in April 1984 spending three days in the capital as a floating exhibition centre for Gotland trade, commerce and tourism. The following year saw attempts to generate additional traffic by early and late season sailings direct from Stockholm to Visby. However, complications arose over tax free sales on board and the experiment was not repeated in subsequent years.

The layout of *Visby*'s accommodation, with cabins forward and the bars, restaurants and other amenities aft, is identical to that of sister ship *Peter Wessel*, described earlier and, unusual in Scandinavian ferries, each also has a 204-seat cinema beneath the car decks which, to some extent, makes up for the lack of large scale conference facilities on board.

With doubts emerging over the future of the Gotland service, efforts to find the ship a new role started as early as the spring of 1987 but

eventually, it became clear that *Visby* would stay put with new operators Gotlandslinjen aiming to build a reputation on better timed sailings plus improved publicity and marketing. Far greater emphasis was also placed on adding style and flair to the *Visby*'s day to day running which was entrusted to Silja Line partners Johnson Line of Stockholm as managers.

Graip

Owner Norstrom & Thulin. **Flag** Swedish. **Operator** Gotlandslinjen. **Route** Oskarhamn-Visby. **Built** Hyundai Shipbuilding, South Korea in 1978, rebuilt by Blohm and Voss, Hamburg, 1987. **Gross tonnage** 18,500. **Net tonnage** 10,500. **Length** 151 m. **Width** 24 m. **Draught** 6 m. **Machinery** 2 Pielstick diesels of 15,200 hp. **Speed** 17 knots. **Passengers** 1,700. **Cabin berths** 400. **Vehicle capacity** 500 cars.

Gotlandslinjen plan to supplement *Visby*'s sailings from Nynashamn with a 320-seat high speed catamaran while the route between Visby and Oskarshamn has been entrusted to the former *Stena Shipper* now renamed *Graip*. One of the Korean-built 'Searunner' series of trailer ferries, it took over the service in January 1988 after a 100 million SKR reconstruction in Hamburg by Blohm and Voss. The vessel received passenger accommodation for 1,700 in an operation similar to those undertaken on former sister ships *Baltic Ferry* and *Nordic Ferry*, now maintaining the Felixstowe-Zeebrugge link for P&O Ferries. The main passenger areas have been built at two levels on the previous container deck, with the addition of a top saloon seating over 200 at a third level. *Graip* still had its original superstructure at the stern and space below has been utilized to house cabins berthing 400. Already nine metres longer than *Visby*, the *Graip*'s width will be increased by stability sponsons to 24 metres, the same as the purpose-built passenger vessel. Even after conversion, the Baltic newcomer has space for 500 cars or 60 lorries.

Chapter 6

The Mediterranean

The Mediterranean, and especially services eminating from Greece, is a kaleidoscope of car ferry evolution, representing several generations of development from Scandinavia, Northern Europe and even Japan with the ships themselves part of a vibrant but fluid scene with complicated ownership arrangements and a tendency for new operators to spring up and sometimes disappear almost as quickly. There is a clear east/west divide within the Mediterranean, the generally long established and well defined pattern of services by Spanish, French and Italian enterprises (some in conjunction with North African associates) contrasting with the rather more cosmopolitan range of ships and services from the Adriatic and further east.

The geographical split is evident too in the various fleets, with those in the western section such as Trasmediterranea of Spain, the French Societie Nationale Maritime Corse Mediterranee (SNCM) with its Tunisian and Algerian partners, as well as the leading Italian companies such as Tirrenia Line and the State Railway's shipping arm, all running fleets consisting largely of modern purpose-built tonnage — and in the case of SNCM a string of vessels of genuine super-ferry proportions. To the east, fast expanding traffic from Italy to Greece, as well as routes from Greek mainland ports to Crete, Cyprus and countless islands in the Dodecanese, support ships of infinite variety — and in some cases comparitive antiquity — and, apart from a pair of former cargo vessels strikingly rebuilt for passenger and vehicle carriage and two mid-1970s Baltic exiles introduced in

1986 and 1987, the jumbo ferry is hardly a serious contender yet.

That is not to say the conversion of smaller ships has lacked style or ingenuity and a number of units originally for short duration crossings have been provided with cabins and placed on international overnight services. The procession to the Mediterranean of ferries in the 5,000–10,000 tons range started in the 1960s when almost every second–hand vessel found a ready buyer in Greece, some of the purchases proving purely speculative with ships only languishing before eventually being broken-up.

Societie Nationale Maritime Corse Mediterranee (SNCM)

France has always placed great emphasis on sea connections between mainland and former North African colonies and the island of Corsica, yet until the mid-1960s the trade was handled by conventional passenger vessels, mostly turbine powered. While one ship, dating from 1959, had side-loading facilities for around 100 cars, it was not until 1966 that a recognizable modern car ferry with stern as well as side-loading capability was introduced on the Corsican service, linking Marseille or Nice with Ajaccio and Bastia.

This was the 5,000 ton *Fred Scamaroni* from the Mediterranean fleet of French Line (Compagnie Generale Transatlantique) which was later re-organized as Cie Generale Transmediterraneene to trade under the Transmed banner until 1976 when SNCM was formed through an amalgamation of Transmed and their principal rivals for North African and Corsican traffic, Marseille-based Compagnie de Navigation Mixte.

The company is now 80 per cent owned by Compagnie Generale Maritime, with the remaining 20 per cent in the hands of French Railways (SNCF) whose influence is reflected in the fare structure. Rates for the sea crossings are broadly similar to those for railway journeys of similar distance in France.

A fleet replacement programme began immediately and in little more than seven years SNCM introduced half a dozen substantial modern car ferries to completely displace earlier tonnage. A larger number of ro-ro trailer ferries came on stream in the same period as SNCM also developed close operating ties on the North African services with the Algerian and Tunisian state companies, CNAN and CTN.

Now SNCM are looking to the future and late in April 1987 contracts were signed with Chantier de l'Atlantique at St. Nazaire for a super-ferry with overnight capacity for 2,300 passengers and space for up to 600 cars which will complete fleet renewals when delivered for the Corsican routes at the end of March 1989.

Napoleon

Owner Society Nationale Maritime Corse Mediterranee. **Flag** French. **Operator** SNCM. **Route** France-Corsica. **Built** Dubigenon Normandie, Nantes, in 1976. **Gross tonnage** 14,918. **Net tonnage** 8,145. **Length** 155 m. **Width** 24.4 m.

Draught 6.1 m. **Machinery** 2 Pielstick diesels of 25,150 hp. **Speed** 23.5 knots. **Passengers** 1,844. **Cabin berths** 1,408. **Vehicle capacity** 500 cars. **Vehicle access** Bow and stern.

SNCM's first priority was to modernize the Corsican fleet. The new *Napoleon* was brought into service in June 1976 and in both size and facilities was much in advance of anything seen previously on the route. It has overnight space for a total of 1,844 passengers compared to just over 1,000 in its predecessor and while the 5,564 ton *Napoleon* of 1959 squeezed in 100 cars, the current ship's twin decks with bow, stern and side access doors comfortably take 500.

Napolean completely overshadowed *Fred Scamaroni* and the smaller vessel was sold before figuring as *Nuits St. Georges* in an unsuccessful 1980 attempt by Olau Line founder Ole Lauritzen to start a new English Channel service between Ramsgate and Dunkirk. Both the ship and facilities at Ramsgate were unsuitable but the route's potential was spotted by Rederi Sally of Finland who came in a year later with Scandinavian tonnage and developed a thriving operation which also involved massive investment in the port of Ramsgate itself.

The first super-ferry for long-established services from the French mainland to Corsica was Napoleon, *completed in 1976 and accommodating over 1,800 passengers* (Antonio Scrimali).

The *Napoleon* carries both first and second class passengers with a total of 618 places in the premier category and 1,226 at second class level, although the main public rooms are generally available and include a 350 seat cinema, both *à la carte* and self-service restaurants and an extensive bar-lounge. Unique to SNCM is accommodation for both first and second class passengers in railway carriage style compartments which are also fully utilized on day sailings when the ship's certificate is reduced to a total of 1,415.

Two Pielstick PC3V engines give *Napoleon* a maximum speed of over 23 knots and this is needed in the summer peak when as many as six return sailings a day are provided from Marseille and Nice to four different Corsican ports by a quartet of intensively worked ferries.

Cyrnos

Owner Societie Nationale Corse-Mediterranee. **Flag** French. **Operator** SNCM. **Route** France-Corsica, France-Sardinia. **Built** Dubigenon Normandie, Nantes, in 1979. **Gross tonnage** 12,625. **Net tonnage** 6,500. **Length** 138.5 m. **Width** 23.0 m. **Draught** 5.9 m. **Machinery** 4 x Pielstick diesels of 22,950 hp. **Speed** 22.9 knots. **Passengers** 1,667. **Cabin berths** 1,074. **Vehicle capacity** 440 cars. **Vehicle access** Bow and stern.

SNCM returned to Dubigenon-Normandie for another new building to join *Napoleon* on the Corsican service but *Cyrnos*, ordered in June 1977 and launched in November 1978, was in no way a sister ship, being almost 20 metres shorter and with completely different internal arrangements. Passenger capacity is slightly smaller than that of *Napoleon* and balance between day and night loadings is altered with this ship equipped to take 1,629 on day sailings and 1,362 overnight.

First class night accommodation for 538 is centred on a complete deck immediately below the service area which is laid-out in an uncomplicated style. There is bar-lounge area forward and side passages lead aft on either beam past a central galley, with a self-service restaurant seating 300, before a further aft lounge for 200 opens on to an outside terrace. Second class berths and compartments also occupy an entire deck before the vehicle deck and platform deck with room for 430 cars.

Cyrnos entered service in May 1979 and with power from four Pielstick diesels producing a top speed of 22 knots is used throughout the year on Corsican services from Marseille where crossing times range from a minimum of 8 hours 30 minutes for the 178 nautical mile journey to Ajaccio, to 10 hours for the 210 miles to Bastia. The shortest 93-mile link between Nice and Calvi takes five hours and there are also seasonal services from Toulon taking

Further new tonnage for the Corsican services of SNCM was provided in 1979 with the completion of Cyrnos *which also figures in summer links between France and Sardinia* (Antonio Scrimali).

from seven to eight-and-a-half hours. At times *Cyrnos* also figures in a summer weekend service from Toulon or Marseille to Porto Torres in Sardinia.

Esterel/Corse

Owner Societie Nationale Maritime Corse-Mediterranee. **Flag** French. **Operator** SNCM. **Route** Esterel: France-Algeria, France-Tunisia, France-Corsica; Corse: France-Corsica. **Built** Dubigenon Normandie, Nantes, in 1981/1983. **Gross tonnage** 12,676. **Net tonnage** 6,850. **Length** 145 m. **Width** 23.3 m. **Draught** 6.3 m. **Machinery** 4 x Pielstick diesels of 27,536 hp. **Speed**

SNCM's practice of building single ships was dropped when Dubigeon Normandie turned out first Esterel *in 1981 and sister vessel* Corse *two years later.* Esterel *figures on North African services while* Corse *is confined to the Corsican routes* (Antonio Scrimali).

23.5 knots. **Passengers** 2,386/2,262. **Cabin berths** 630. **Vehicle capacity** 700 cars. **Vehicle access** Bow, stern and side.

SNCM finally abandoned their policy of building single ships when going to Dubigenon-Normandie for a pair of vessels capable of use on either the Corsican or North African services. The lead ship was commissioned as *Esterel* in May 1981 and was followed by identical sister *Corse* in time for the summer peak of 1983, its first sailings taking place early in June.

A main feature was the inclusion of three full vehicle decks capable of accommodating 700 cars and for the first time in its modern car ferries SNCM placed passenger accommodation beneath the vehicle decks with both second class compartments and a first class pullman lounge. The latter type of reserved seating predominates, both classes having large separate lounges of seats with tables. The arrangement results in only the bar and brasserie, a 150-seat cinema and small disco being available for all passengers.

Pielstick machinery giving a top speed of 22.5 knots was selected for the two ships and *Esterel* has proved especially versatile. 1986 operations were typical with use to Corsica and on both of the North African services, supplementing SNCM's smaller regular ship, *Liberte*, built in 1980, and the 11,000 ton *Habib* of CTN on the 24-hour crossings to Tunisia. *Esterel* also ran on the slightly longer Algerian route in which *Liberte* also figures along with smaller ships from the CNAN fleet.

Not surprisingly, *Corse* has been used almost exclusively to Corsica as part of a four-ship peak season SNCM line-up completed by *Napoleon*, *Cyrnos* and the Italian-built 7,740 ton *Provence* of 1974, which is especially useful being equipped with ramps forward and aft on either side in addition to the normal bow and stern openings.

Ile de Beaute

Owner Societie Nationale Maritime Corse-Mediterranee. **Flag** French. **Operator** SNCM. **Route** France-Corsica. **Builder** Chantier de l'Atlantique, St. Nazaire, ordered April 1987 for delivery on 31 March 1989. **Gross tonnage** Not available. **Net tonnage** Not available. **Length** 160 m. **Width** Not available. **Draught** Not available. **Machinery** 4 x Pielstick diesels. **Speed** 23 knots. **Passengers** 2,300. **Cabin berths** Not available. **Vehicle capacity** 600/800 cars. **Vehicle access** Bow and stern.

SNCM were known to be working in 1985–6 on plans for a final large ferry to complete the replacement programme and enable the *Provence* to be phased-out of Corsican schedules, yet it was not until late in April 1987 that confirmation emerged of an order to the Chantier de l'Atlantique yard for what the company claimed will be the largest European car ferry with space for as many as 800 on three decks, together with 2,300 passengers. At 160 metres, however, the new vessel, scheduled for March 1989 delivery, is only slightly longer than the *Napoleon* and not as long as a number of recent Baltic vessels, or the Townsend Thoresen 'Pride' class sisters.

British Ferries

One of the first moves made by Bermuda-based Sea Containers after the purchase of Sealink in July 1985 was the announcement of a weekly cruise-ferry service in the eastern Mediterranean from Venice to Istanbul and back. The route, a logical extension of the Venice-Simplon-Orient Express train operation already being successfully run by another Sea-Co subsidiary company, was aimed at both round trip cruise passengers and ordinary ro-ro traffic over individual sectors.

There was early speculation that the route would be covered by the German-built one-time Viking Line ferry *Earl Granville*, which had been expensively refitted early in 1985 for a re-vamped but unprofitable Channel Island service.

Although a former Baltic ferry did inaugurate the route from Venice in May 1986, Sea Containers were looking for a ship with larger passenger and vehicle capcity and bought the eleven-year-old *Silja Star* from Silja Line partners Finland Steamship Company (EFFOA). This vessel was refitted in Bremerhaven before a voyage directly to the Mediterranean via the English Channel but, surprisingly, without any calls in British ports.

The ship, renamed *Orient Express*, was aimed particularly at the West German and North American markets and managed to produce satisfactory first season returns despite a very substantial loss of transatlantic bookings for Medieterranean cruising and European tourism as a whole because of fears of terrorism after hijacking of the cruise liner *Achille Lauro* and other incidents. For 1987 the weekly circuit from Venice to Piraeus and Istanbul, returning via Kusadasi in Southern Turkey, Patmos and Katakolon was unchanged and consistently high load factors were achieved.

Orient Express

Owner Sea Containers. **Flag** Bermuda. **Operator** British Ferries. **Route** Venice-Istanbul. **Built** Dubigenon, Normandie, Nantes, in 1975. **Gross**

tonnage 12,343. **Net tonnage** 6,198. **Length** 152.4 m. **Width** 22 m. **Draught** 5.8 m. **Machinery** 4 Pielstick diesels of 24,000 hp. **Speed** 21 knots. **Passengers** 800. **Cabin berths** 747. **Vehicle capacity** 240. **Vehicle access** Bow and stern. **Former names** *Bore Star* (Bore Line 1975–80); *Silja Star* (EFFOA 1980–85). **Sister vessels** *Dana Gloria* (DFDS); *Pegasus* (Epirotiki Line).

Orient Express, launched on 30 January 1975 as *Bore Star*, was the lead ship of three built at Nantes by Dubigenon-Normandie for the trio of companies then forming the Silja Line consortium. The ship was delivered in December of the same year and placed on the Stockholm-Helsinki route which it mainly served right through until the early 1980s and the arrival of the first of the Silja jumbo ferries. By then Bore Line had withdrawn from passenger operations and *Bore Star* was bought in July 1980 by one of the remaining Silja partners, EFFOA. Renamed *Silja Star*, she continued on the Helsinki run until displaced by the new *Silvia Regina* from April 1982, then switching to the Turku-Stockholm route.

Again, it was not long before new tonnage was taking shape and *Silja Star* finally stood down at the end of 1985, the last of the French-built trio to operate in the Baltic. A sale to Sea Containers for a reported $16.5 million had already been finalized and the vessel went to Lloyd Werft for an extended overhaul including the upgrading of cabins, and other major works such as the construction of an outdoor swimming pool aft. It emerged from the yard in an adapted form of the livery applied to Sealink's fleet operating in British waters and re-equipped to take a total of 800 passengers,

Below and overleaf   *Three stages in the career of a ferry built to cope with the Baltic winter ice and now operating in the rather warmer conditions of the Eastern Mediterranean. Built as* Bore Star *in 1975, the 12,343 ton vessel remained within the Silja Line organization when brought by EFFOA and renamed* Silja Star *in 1980. Six years later there was a Mediterranean debut as* Orient Express *(Anders Ahlerup/British Ferries).*

747 berthed, instead of the previous 1,400 for day sailings.

Orient Express, registered in Bermuda, arrived at Venice in April 1986 and, prior to the 3 May maiden sailing, made a trip over the entire route to test the berthing facilities and also dispel doubts that the vessel was too large to use the Corinth Canal by completing a trial transit — although it was a fairly tight squeeze with only a few feet of clearance on either beam. The ship passes through the canal on the eastbound sailing at first light each Monday but it is hardly a leisurely pleasure cruise in the first section of the weekly circuit following a Saturday evening departure from Venice, for full power from a quartet of French-built Pielsticks is needed to give a speed of over 20 knots in order to reach Piraeus at breakfast time on Monday. While the later scheduling is more relaxed, the ferry element is not forgotten.

Istanbul is advertised as the final destination of the service but the city boasts no ro-ro facilities and the *Orient Express* actually berths on the Asian side of the Bosphorus near Uskudar during a ten-hour stop-over. In the return direction the call at Piraeus is omitted although a stop at Katakolon, not far from Patras, provides some scope for the vessel to pick up Greece-Italy vehicle traffic.

Orient Express completed its first season towards the end of October 1986 having carried 17,500 passengers and then crossed the Atlantic to commence a winter charter in the Caribbean involving a series of fourteen one-week cruises from Antigua for an American operator. However, bookings failed to come up to expectations and half the trips were cancelled, the ship returning early to the Mediterranean in January 1987 for overhaul at Venice. Before starting a second summer on the Istanbul service during April 1987, the *Orient Express* undertook a series of educational cruises from mid-March for the British specialist company, Schools Abroad.

The vessel remained on the Istanbul service during the summer of 1987 before switching base to the Canary Islands for a series of week-long cruises from Teneriffe to Maderia, Lan-

Below Orient Express, *here arriving at Piraeus in June 1986, represents an interesting variation of the colours applied to Sealink British Ferries vessels rather nearer home* (L.W.C. Lamers).

From passenger liner to ferry, the veteran Mediterranean Star *shows little change externally from its days in the Union-Castle fleet. The vessel was prominent in the development of the Italy–Greece ferry trade in the late 1970s* (Antonio Scrimali).

zarote, Agadir, Laayone and Las Palmas lasting until early in April 1988.

Karageorgis Lines

In the early 1970s Greek shipowner Michail A. Karageorgis saw the potential for a year-round passenger and vehicle service between Greece and Italy but in the absence of suitable existing tonnage and, as a cheaper alternative to new construction, he took the then rather unusual step of buying conventional cargo vessels and totally rebuilding two of them before launching the Karageorgis Lines route from Patras to Ancona in 1972.

Efthymaidis Lines had converted a couple of former tankers into side-loading car ferries for use between Greece and Italy in 1966 but the antecendence of the Swedish-built sisters was still very apparent with most of the passenger accommodation positioned between the forward island bridge and the aft superstructure. The Karageorgis approach was to rebuild everything apart from the bare hull and machinery with designer John Bannerburg, already widely known for his work on Cunard's *Queen Elizabeth 2*, giving full expression to futuristic outlines that still appear modern after two decades of service.

The pattern of service, with one vessel running year-round and the second introduced for a five month summer stint, has been sup-

plemented on occasions by the addition of other tonnage in the peak period and for several years Karageorgis used the veteran *Mediterranean Star*, built at Belfast by Harland and Wolff in 1950 as *Bloemfontain Castle*. After almost ten years on Union-Castle Line's South African routes the vessel was bought by Chandris and used on conventional liner services to Australia, and cruising, until converted into a side-loading ferry for 250 cars and introduced to the Greece-Italy run as *Patris* in 1976. When Karageorgis bought the 18,259 ton ship in 1979 it not only provided useful capacity boost but also eliminated a major competitor, Chandris taking no further part in the Mediterranean ferry trade. An earlier Karageorgis purchase in 1980 was the former Silja Line ferry *Svea Regina* which became *Mediterranean Star* but proved too small and went through several changes of ownership before finally reaching Florida and a role in the Sea Escape day cruise operation as *Scandinavian Sky*.

In 1983, as mentioned in an earlier chapter, Karageorgis chartered *Wasa Star* in place of *Mediterranean Star*. The old-timer which first ran for Karageorgis as *Mediteranean Island* until 1981, did not return to the route in 1984, but she was back in commission in 1986 when chartered to maintain a weekly summer circuit from Greece to Egypt, finally being sold to Pakistani breakers in 1987.

Mediterranean Sea

Owner Mikar Ltd, Limassol. **Flag** Cyprus. **Operator** Karageorgis Lines. **Route** Patras-Ancona. **Built** Vickers Armstrong, Newcastle, 1953; rebuilt by Alliance Navigation, Perama, 1972. **Gross tonnage** 16,384. **Net tonnage** 9,330. **Length** 164.7 m. **Width** 21.6 m. **Draught** 6.3 m. **Machinery** 2 Doxford diesels of 12,650 hp. **Speed** 18 knots. **Passengers** 854. **Cabin berths** 854. **Vehicle capacity** 350 cars. **Vehicle access** Side. **Former name** *City of Exeter* (Ellerman Lines 1953–71).

Michail Karageorgis actually bought four cargo vessels from Ellerman Lines of London for conversion into ferries but only the 1953 pair *City of Exeter* and *City of York* were rebuilt, with the *City of Port Elizabeth*, dating from 1952 and allocated the name *Mediterranean Sun*, being sold for scrap in 1979 after lying untouched in Piraeus. These vessels, and the identical *City of Durban* (1954), also scrapped, were three-island cargo/passenger ships of 13,400 gross tons, built by Vickers-Armstrong on the Tyne

Still looking strikingly modern more than a decade after almost total reconstruction from a cargo vessel, Mediterranean Sea *runs throughout the year between Ancona and Patras. The side vehicle entrance can be easily identified as the ship approaches the Greek port at the end of a sailing* (Antonio Scrimali).

and used for Ellerman's routes from Britain to ports in South and East Africa. The largest ships in the Ellerman fleet, they had high quality accommodation for about 100 passengers and were designed to make the London-Capetown passage in sixteen days.

City of Exeter was the first to be reconstructed, emerging from the Alliance yard at Perama, near Piraeus, as *Mediterranean Sea*, registered in Cyprus at Limassol and totally unrecognizable from the traditional cargo ship it had once been. The ship was given a canary yellow hull, streamlined white superstructure and a single stump mast positioned above the bridge and ahead of the striking funnel. Accommodation for 854 passengers is provided on three decks in a range of cabins, including what Karageorgis claims to be the only true 'de luxe' category on the route, as well as two, three, four and six-berth units with private facilities.

The Promenade Deck has first class space forward with a lounge bar looking out over a glass-screened lido with swimming pool. A tourist class pool and sun deck is situated aft as well as the main tourist lounge area. There are separate first and tourist class restaurants towards the stern at the next level down and, interestingly, the galley is positioned right at the stern. The original pair of Doxford main engines were retained and the hold space forward of the machinery has been adapted as a garage for up to 350 cars and although loading is by side ports there is clearance to take coaches or as many as 25 lorries.

Mediterranean Sea opened the Patras-

Above   *Another major conversion job in the 1970s produced* Mediterranean Sky *to provide summer support for* Mediterranean Sea *on the Karageogis Italy–Greece connection* (Antonio Scrimali).

Below and below right   Mediterranean Sky *in dry dock for underwater repainting at Perama in June 1986* (Antonio Scrimali).

Ancona service in 1972 and has always been the route's principal ferry running on a year-round basis. In 1987 the vessel departed Ancona on Wednesday and Saturday on a 33-hour schedule to Patras with return departures on Monday and Friday, all sailings having coach links to Athens.

Mediterranean Sky

Owner Pandiestra Oceanica Navigation. **Flag** Greece. **Operator** Karageorgis Lines. **Route** Patras-Ancona. **Built** Vickers Armstrong, Newcastle, 1953; rebuilt by Alliance Navigation, Perama, 1974. **Gross tonnage** 14,941. **Net tonnage** 8,470. **Length** 164.7 m. **Width** 21.6 m. **Draught** 6.3 m. **Machinery** 2 Doxford diesels of 12,650 hp. **Speed** 18 knots. **Passengers** 800. **Cabin berths** 800. **Vehicle capacity** 300. **Vehicle access** Side. **Former name** *City of York* (Ellerman Line 1953–71).

Once *Mediterranean Sea* was in service, work commenced on *City of York*, although in external appearance and the interior layout it was anything but a copy of the earlier conversion. *Mediterranean Sky* was intended specifically for the summer supporting role and received

slightly less streamlining of the upperworks and less extensive accommodation in an exercise completed in time for a 1974 debut on the Ancona route.

Berths were provided for 800, again on three decks, and with a selection of cabin grades from 'de luxe' on the Promenade Deck complete with reserved lounge, to four and six-berth combinations on the Upper and Main Decks. There is a single swimming pool and sun deck aft on the Promenade Deck which also includes a general bar saloon, snack bar and tavern. The restaurant and galley are positioned aft, as in the *Mediterranean Sea*.

The garage area is rather smaller than in the previous conversion and takes around 300 cars through side ports but once again the Doxford machinery was retained and is capable of a speed of 18 knots. *Mediterranean Sky* usually operates from late May until the end of October covering Sunday and Wednesday trips from Patras and Monday and Friday return sailings ex-Ancona.

Minoan Lines

After making its name linking Crete with the Greek mainland and expanding with judicious purchases of modern medium-sized Scandinavian tonnage, Minoan Lines bought a Japanese ferry to compete for a share of the expanding Greece-Italy ferry market, introducing the 9,000 ton *El Greco* between Patras and Ancona via Igoumenitsa in 1981.

By then the Crete services were in the hands of *Ariadne*, bought in 1975 (and previously one of the first Tor Line twins, built in Germany in 1967 as *Tor Hollandia*) and *Knossos* (1966), bought from Swedish-Lloyd in 1978 after a lengthy spell on the Tilbury-Gothenburg service as *Saga*. Initially these ships were on the year-round Piraeus-Heraklion route while Minoan Line's pioneer unit, the converted tanker *Minos* ran between Piraeus and Chania.

Knossos was joined on the Heraklion route in 1985 by its much-travelled near sister the former *Folkliner*, *Olau Finn*, *Finnpartner* and *Hispania* which became *Festos*, releasing *Ariadne* to re-open the connection with Chania which had been dropped following disposal of the side-loading *Minos*. Then, towards the end of 1986, Minoan Lines acted to strengthen their Italian service by the advance purchase of TT Line's *Robin Hood* which was delivered in March 1987 and refitted before making first sailings from Patras as *Fedra*.

Fedra

Owner Minoan Lines. **Flag** Greek. **Operator** Minoan Lines. **Route** Patras-Ancona. **Built** Werft Nobiskrug, Rendsburg, in 1974. **Gross tonnage** 12,528. **Net tonnage** 6,903. **Length** 148.9 m. **Width** 23.3 m. **Draught** 5.5 m. **Machinery** 2 Pielstick diesels of 15,300 hp. **Speed** 21 knots. **Passengers** 1,800. **Cabin berths** 712. **Vehicle capacity** 470 cars. **Vehicle access** Bow and stern. **Former names** *Peter Pan* (TT Line 1974–85); *Robin Hood* (TT Line 1986–7). **Sister vessel** *Abel Tasman* (Transport of Tasmania), formerly *Nils Holgersson* (TT Line 1975–84).

Just as most first generation car ferries found ready buyers when placed on the second–hand market after replacement by larger units, the early jumbos have been in even greater demand as was demonstrated by the ease with which TT Line disposed of *Nils Holgersson* and *Peter Pan*, vessels which were the mainstay of their services for over ten years from the mid-1970s. While the former went to Australian waters, its identical sister, latterly used on the Baltic as *Robin Hood*, became the largest of the Minoan Lines' fleet when introduced in 1987 as *Fedra*.

Ordered from Werft Nobiskrug in 1973, the

Peter Pan *and* Nils Holgersson *steaming abreast in a carefully stage-managed TT Line publicity shot from the late 1970s* (TT Line)

Peter Pan was launched at Rendsburg on the Kiel Canal in February 1974 and completed in May of the same year in time for a full summer of service on the TT route from Travemunde to Trelleborg. The *Nils Holgersson* was launched in October the same year and completed in April 1975. Accommodating 1,800 passengers in a single class with berths for more than 700 in 189 double and 83 four berth cabins, these ships certainly provided some of the highest quality facilities seen in Northern Europe and it says a lot for their design that in neither case were major alterations considered necessary following sale. The main services are all positioned on the Restaurant Deck with separate buffet and *à la carte* restaurants, an extensive self-service cafeteria, plenty of bar and lounge space and shops. Additional amenities beneath the vehicle decks (which have room for almost 500 cars) include a good size indoor swimming pool with saunas and solarium.

TT Line's present giant ships had hardly been ordered in 1984 when *Nils Holgersson* was bought by the Tasmanian Government and refitted in Germany before making the long delivery voyage south and an introduction on the fourteen hour Bass Strait crossing from Melbourne to East Devonport in Tasmania as *Abel Tasman*.

Above Peter Pan *became* Robin Hood *for its final fourteen months on TT's Travemunde–Trelleborg service and is seen at the German port in May 1986* (Author).

Below Fedra *entered service on the Minoan Lines Patras–Ancona route in June 1987, joining a smaller Japanese-built ferry. Here she is seen in the Kiel Canal on 20 March 1987, the day after Minoan Lines accepted delivery following an overhaul by Werft Nobiskrug* (Gerhard Fiebiger).

While her sister ship went to the Mediterranean, Nils Holgersson's *new stamping ground is even further afield, on the Bass Strait service between Australia and Tasmania as* Abel Tasman (Trans Tasmania Line).

Peter Pan continued on the Germany-Sweden route opposite different chartered stand-in ferries and was renamed *Robin Hood* in January 1986 to free the original name for the first of TT's 31,000 ton giants completed five months later. *Robin Hood* remained until after the new *Nils Holgersson* was delivered in March 1987.

After completing final sailings for TT Line, *Robin Hood* returned to the yard of builders Werft Nobiskrug at Rendsburg on the Kiel Canal for a refit and was renamed *Fedra* before being officially handed over to Minoan Lines on 19 March. Work did not include external repainting and *Fedra* left with little more than the TT Line hull markings and bow badge painted out and retaining just the higher yellow flash on the funnel. Following arrival in the Eastern Mediterranean there was more attention in Piraeus with application of the full Minoan Lines livery, including the actual ship's name in Greek script.

Fedra shared the Patras-Ancona summer service with *El Greco* and continued to operate two return sailings a week throughout the winter months. A more intensive peak season programme was announced for 1988 with Minoan Lines adding further tonnage to serve Corfu from Italy. *Fedra* and the other vessels were also equipped with gaming facilities, the onboard casinos giving passengers the opportunity for a flutter on roulette and blackjack for the first time.

Chapter 7

Implications of disaster

The safety standards achieved by ferry companies large and small are remarkable in view of the ever increasing size of the ships themselves and, especially on high density routes such as the short dash across the English Channel or principal overnight services, the sheer volume of passengers handled. The record of ferries compares most favourably with other forms of transport on land or in the air, yet public confidence, in Britain at least, was severely tested after the events of a cold night in March 1987 when the seven-year-old Townsend Thoresen vessel *Herald of Free Enterprise* left Zeebrugge bound for Dover with, almost unbelievably, its inner and outer bow doors left gaping open.

Many months later, the television pictures and newspaper coverage of the resulting catastrophe, which claimed over 190 lives, are still chillingly vivid, and although it was quickly established that the disaster stemmed from human and procedural shortcomings rather than anything mechanical, it brought safety and design questions into sharper and more immediate focus than ever before. Whilst not all of the findings of investigations into some previous maritime incidents involving this type of ship have been acted upon, on this occasion the British Government and Department of Transport demonstrated a determination to implement quickly the recommendations of a public inquiry into the tragedy.

Less than a month after the findings of the 29-day London hearing before Mr Justice Sheen were announced, the Government directed that operators of both British and foreign tonnage using United Kingdom ports must, by 1 November 1988, equip the bridge of every vessel with vehicle deck door indicator lights, closed-circuit television monitors, improved emergency lighting and other items. There will also be research into roll-on/roll-off ferry design with emphasis on the feasibility of transverse bulkheads – the large expanse of undivided deck space only a few feet above the water line being regarded by some experts as a potentially dangerous feature in this type of vessel.

On 6 March 1987, the 7,950 ton *Herald of Free Enterprise* had hardly cleared the outer harbour at Zeebrugge before sea water rushed in through the unclosed doors to swamp the main vehicle deck and cause a rapid loss of stability. The ship lurched first to port and then fell to starboard before coming to rest on its side, half submerged on a sand bar and just out of the main Channel. The sand bank kept a substantial part of the wreck above the water and this factor, together with the close proximity of the shore, enabled a remarkable rescue operation to be completed in darkness by the Belgian authorities although, tragically, 189 people drowned.

The outer shell doors fitted in the bows of the *Herald of Free Enterprise* and its two 'Spirit' class sister vessels are of a rather unusual design and cannot be seen from the wheelhouse or bridge wings. In most other ferries bow doors are visibile either because they open outwards in butterfly wing fashion, or because a bow visor is raised. As built, the 'Spirit' trio had no door indicator lights on their bridges and the

Herald of Free Enterprise *moving astern out of Calais in 1984. The largely enclosed passenger accommodation made escape more difficult for passengers after the capsize in March 1987 and one of the recommendations of the public enquiry was that the windows of such areas should include more easily operated emergency exits* (Author).

public inquiry also established that Townsend Thoresen did not employ a positive reporting system to confirm door closure prior to departure.

Since 1984, the installation of warning lights has been obligatory in all new British ro-ro ships and any lengthened or rebuilt. Under this legislation the Townsend Thoreson ferries *Free Enterprise VI, Free Enterprise VII, Viking Venturer* and *Viking Valiant*, which received doors similar to those of the *Herald of Free Enterprise* when extensively enlarged in Germany in 1985-86, were equipped with bridge lights. There was a similar facility in the former trailer ships *Baltic Ferry* and *Nordic Ferry* even before they were converted to a passenger role and switched to the Felixstowe-Zeebrugge run in 1986.

Confirmation that Townsend Thoresen were using ferries lacking even a rudimentary warning light system staggered major Scandinavian operators such as DFDS, Stena Line, Viking Line

and Silja Line whose vessels have boasted elaborate electronic bridge displays for a number of years, with more recent units having the additional back-up of television surveillance.

The inquiry report found that the loss of *Herald of Free Enterprise* was caused by the negligence of its captain, the chief officer, the assistant bosun and Townsend Car Ferries as owners and operators. The certificate of competence of the master, Captain David Lewry, was suspended for a year — although at the time of writing his appeal against this decision has still to be heard. The certificate of chief officer Mr Leslie Sabel was suspended for two years and the judge slammed Townsend Thoresen's senior management for what he described as a 'disease of sloppiness' running through the whole organization.

The senior master of *Herald of Free Enterprise*, Captain John Kirby, was also criticized for accepting defective standing orders from the company and for not issuing his own clear and concise instructions about the operation of the bow doors. But, said Mr Justice Sheen, the company had ignored major complaints from some captains about safety and operational matters, and had reacted to their suggestions in a manner which 'displayed an absence of any sense of responsibility'.

Evidence heard by the inquiry included allegations that Townsend Thoreson ferries sailed on occasions with more than the number of passengers allowed by their certificates, false entries being made in the log to cover discrepancies. It was also claimed that the draught of the vessel was often not checked prior to departures, with more ficticious entries made on official records.

On the fateful night, *Herald of Free Enterprise* had taken water into its forward ballast tanks to ensure an optimum fit with the Zeebrugge linkspan and was still bow down on departure. This undoubtedly increased the amount of water which entered the vehicle deck in such quantities and quickly destroyed stability. At the same time as acknowledging that any measures to improve the survivability of ferries would inevitably add to construction and equipment costs, the inquiry called for all possibilities of keeping damaged ships afloat longer to be investigated.

Areas highlighted included the need for improved pumping systems to remove water from the vehicle decks; a possible increase in the freeboard of ferries to put main vehicle decks at a greater height above the water line; and a

Following the tragic accident on 6 March 1987, Herald of Free Enterprise *is seen capsized outside the harbour of Zeebrugge with vessels from Smit International close by prior to the start of the salvage operation* (Fotoflite).

discouragement of slab-sided ferry designs which eliminate escape routes and invariably places lifeboat stations a very considerable height above the water. *Herald of Free Enterprise* and its sisters have lifeboats located in a mid-hull position and also a system of sophisticated aircraft-type escape chutes, yet disaster overtook the ship so quickly that all were of no avail.

The report did question the value of lifeboats in a rapid capsize situation and suggested that in their place a large number of life rafts could be carried to advantage — a trend already apparent in the more recent Baltic new buildings such as the Silja Line twins *Svea* and *Wellamo*, TT Line's sisters *Peter Pan* and *Nils Holgersson*, and the Polish-built Stena Line pairing of *Stena Germanica* and *Stena Scandinavica*. On the North Sea, the DFDS flagship *Dana Anglia* all but dispensed with lifeboats a decade ago, and a similar policy was adopted by North Sea Ferries when the impressive *Norsea* and *Norsun* were introduced on the Hull-Rotterdam route in 1987.

More difficult to overcome are problems posed by the huge expanses of vehicle deck space on modern ferries, and Mr Justice Sheen had to admit that any division of these areas by transverse bulkheads 'could constitute a grave penalty against the operation of ferry for its intended purpose'. Nevertheless he advocated an exercise into the feasibility of fixed or movable bulkheads and their commercial implications.

Stena Line's latest tonnage follows a trend away from traditional lifeboats with Stena Danica *typical of many modern ferries where only a small number of boats is provided and the space saved is devoted to life rafts* (Author).

Subsequently it was claimed by German ship-builders Schichau Unterweser AG that movable bulkheads could have been fitted in four ferries they re-built for Townsend Thoresen in Bremerhaven during 1985 and 1986, at the seemingly modest cost of £160,000 per ship.

The viability of permanent or portable bulkheads and their effect on the operation of ferries in relation to turn-round times in port forms part of a £1 million research programme financed by a government grant. Also included are model tests to look into methods of improving stability of existing ferries in a review of rules for trimming ballast tanks.

The loss of *Herald of Free Enterprise* was the greatest disaster to overtake the British ferry industry since the 2,694 ton stern loading Irish Sea motor vessel *Princess Victoria* was overwhelmed. This happened on 31 January 1953 in one of the worst storms ever recorded on the North Channel during a crossing between Stranraer and Larne. A total of 128 drowned and only 34 passengers and 10 crew were saved after mountainous waves broke open the stern

doors, flooded the car deck and continued to break over the seven-year-old ship before it finally sank.

Lack of radio communications was blamed as a contributory cause of confusion in the early stages of the rescue operation, and improvements to the design of vehicle deck doors in subsequent British ferries was another outcome of the tragedy.

Capsizing has been the most frequent cause of ferry losses in recent times with vessels turning turtle when taking in water after collision damage — as with the Townsend Thoresen freight ferry *European Gateway* lost off Felixstowe in 1982 — or, in extreme cases, through stability problems caused by bad loading of vehicles. During the 'Herald' inquiry it was said that a spot check at one British port showed 13 per cent of lorries joining a ferry sailing were overloaded and in his findings Mr Justice Sheen called for weigh bridges to be included in the design of ferry ramps to enable the weight of vehicles to be accurately checked.

In the interim, ferry companies were advised to add 13 per cent to the declared weight of lorries and the judge also described as outmoded the practice of assessing every laden car as weighing one tonne. He thought a figure of 1.25 tonnes should be adopted and as accurate reading of draught marks often proved impossible in darkness or choppy conditions, it was also suggested that depth gauges should be fitted to ferries to give precise information to officers prior to each sailing.

Spot checks on ferry door mechanisms brought in at British ports by the Department of Transport immediately after the Zeebrugge disaster were later extended into a more broadly-based series of random checks to ensure that a whole range of statutory requirements was being observed. Loading, stability and numbers of passengers being among the main points covered.

More efficient counting of passengers and the possibility of boarding cards being issued are other areas in which there have been calls for action. However, pressure groups do often fail to appreciate the difference between the short passage ferry operations and the longer type of crossings, usually made all or in part overnight. With the latter, when cabin accommodation is sold detailed information is collected, and many companies now use sophisticated computer booking systems. TT Line, for example, have so refined the art that cabin key cards are individually produced for each crossing and carry the passenger's name.

But airport style check-in systems for Dover or centres such as the Oresund shuttle's ports or Helsingor or Helsingborg, which handle several million passengers a year and have developed the shore facilities to process travellers from terminal to ferry as quickly as possible, are easier discussed than implemented. The imposition of further controls would almost certainly affect efficient running of these ports and the true multi-purpose routes like the 'Bee Line' from Puttgarden in Germany to the Danish port of Rodby between which the majority of crossings take foot passengers, private cars and road freight vehicles in addition to passenger railway coaches and freight wagons.

Much as the loss of *Herald of Free Enterprise* administered a serious shock to the shipping system as a whole, the fact remains that a properly run modern car ferry is among the safest of all forms of transport. Perhaps not all of the inquiry's findings will be acted upon, yet there are already sufficient signs of positive action to suggest that lasting lessons are being learned. Overall, the advances could well be of similar significance to those affecting ocean going passenger vessels following the loss of the *Titanic*.

Below *The second of P&O's English Channel super-ferries* Pride of Calais *arriving in Dover on 1 December 1987 at the end of a delivery voyage from Bremerhaven. The vessel went into service three days later and has the same bow doors as the ill-fated* Herald of Free Enterprise *but boasts sophisticated new safety features including vehicle and passenger door indicator lights and a closed circuit television system with bridge monitors. In addition, all P&O Ferries masters now go through a three phase system of airline style pre-departure checks and before each voyage begins there is a public address confirmation to passengers that the doors are closed and the vessel is ready for sea (P&O Ferries).*

Author's Acknowledgements

The passing of the classic steam-powered passenger ferry is regretted mainly for reasons of nostalgia and while the smooth, vibration-free travel sensation offered at their best might be missed, modern successors are of a size and provide facilities on a scale almost beyond comprehension as little as twenty years ago. The super-ferry of the late 1980s is much more than a floating garage and I hope to have conveyed something of their special attraction and background in the preceeding pages.

Operators have given great assistance in the preparation of the book and this has been more than matched by the reception I received afloat during sailings covering the vast majority of the vessels featured. My special thanks go to Nigel Lingard and Neil Cooper (DFDS Seaways), Case Rietkerk (Olau Line UK), Tony Farrell (North Sea Ferries), Hans Haggman (Silja Line), Inger Lekblad (Stena Line) and David Sayer (Karageorgis Line) for their unfailing help and encouragement. I am also indebted to the production team of Patrick Stephens Ltd for providing facilities to constantly update text and pictures to include major items of information from the vibrant and constantly changing international ferry scene right up to the end of 1987.

All photographs are acknowledged where they appear and special appreciation is due to Anders Ahlerup of Sweden, Antonio Scrimali of Italy, and Steffen Wierauch and Gerhard Fiebiger of West Germany for their contributions — together with those of my associate Scott Dennison who also provided invaluable help with manuscript preparation. Technical information in 'Super-ferries' has been checked with the excellent annual 'Guide' and 'Designs' publications by my friends of Marine Trading at Halmstad, Sweden, and final thanks go to Alan Bates, Editor of *ABC Passenger Shipping Guide* for allowing the reproduction of maps of ferry routes.

Russell Plummer   December 1987.

Index

(Names of Super-ferries in capitals, other vessels lower case)